How to Use the Fiscal Surplus

What is the Optimal Size of Government?

EDITED BY HERBERT GRUBEL

The Fraser Institute

Vancouver   British Columbia   Canada

1998

Printed in Canada.

Canadian Cataloguing in Publication Data

Main entry under title:
How to use the fiscal surplus

   Papers from a conference held in Ottawa, December 3, 1997.
   Includes bibliographical references.
   ISBN 0-88975-190-0

   1. Fiscal policy--Canada--Congresses.   I. Grubel, Herbert G., 1934-
II. Fraser Institute (Vancouver, B.C.)

HJ793.H68 1998   339.5'23'0971   C98-911145-8

Contents

About the Authors

JOHNNY C.P. CHAO is a recent graduate of Simon Fraser University and holds a BBA degree in Business Administration, with a joint major in Economics. He is now a graduate student in the department of Economics at Simon Fraser University. His particular areas of concentration are corporate finance, securities analysis, international trade theory, and the analysis of macro-economic policies.

JEAN J. CHAREST holds a Law degree from the University of Sherbrooke and was called to the Quebec Bar in 1981. First elected to the Parliament in 1984, he was appointed Assistant Deputy Speaker of the House of Commons shortly thereafter. In June 1986, Mr. Charest was appointed Minister of State for Youth and two years later he also assumed the portfolio of Minister of State for Fitness and Amateur Sport. In 1988, he was re-elected and in 1989 the role of Deputy Leader of the Government in the House of Commons was added to his other responsibilities. In 1990, Jean Charest was appointed Chairman of the Special House of Commons Committee on Priorities and Planning and the new Committee on Canadian Unity and Constitutional Negotiations. In June 1993, Jean Charest finished second at the PC Leadership Convention and shortly after was appointed Deputy Prime Minister of Canada and Minister of Industry and Science. He was re-elected for a third consecutive term on October 25, 1993. On December 14, 1993, Jean Charest was appointed Leader of the Progressive Conservative Party of Canada and on April 29, 1995, delegates to the 1995 National Meeting of the Progressive Conservative Party confirmed his leadership. Later in 1995, Jean Charest was named vice-President of the NO Committee for the Quebec referendum campaign. On April 30, Jean Charest became leader of the Liberal Party of Quebec.

STOCKWELL B. DAY is the Provincial Treasurer and Acting Premier of the Government of Alberta. Stockwell Day attended the University of Victoria in Victoria, British Columbia, received training in auctioneering and business in British Columbia and Alberta and also took counselling and ministerial training in Alberta. In business, he has been active in Day's Auction Sales and as a contractor supplying commercial interiors. His community work includes serving as Administrator and Assistant

Pastor at the Bentley Christian School from 1978 to 1985, working on Teen Challenge Ministries, and serving as an education consultant. Stockwell Day has been involved in a number of community activities including fund-raising for local boards and associations and serving as a member of the Red Deer Rotary Club and the Red Deer Branch of the Royal Canadian Legion. Mr. Day was first elected to serve as the Member of the Legislative assembly for Red Deer-North in May 1986. He was re-elected in subsequent elections in March 1989, June 1993 and March 1997. Mr. Day was appointed Provincial Treasurer on March 26, 1997.

ERNIE EVES is Deputy Premier and Minister of Finance for the province of Ontario. He was appointed to these positions on June 26, 1995. As Minister of Finance, Mr. Eves is responsible for Ontario's fiscal and economic policies, the management of provincial finances, and the allocation of a budget of approximately $50 billion. He is also responsible for the development and administration of major tax statutes, and the regulation of Ontario's financial institutions. Mr. Eves is a member of the Policy and Priorities Board of Cabinet and the Vice-Chair of the Management Board of Cabinet, which is responsible for reviewing all government spending.

Mr. Eves was first elected to the Ontario Legislature in 1981 as the member for the riding of Parry Sound and has represented that constituency continuously since that time. He has extensive legislative experience, having served in the Cabinet of former Premier Frank Miller as Minister of Community and Social Services and Minister of Skills Development. He has also been Provincial Secretary for Resources Development, and Parliamentary Assistant to the Minister of Education, Colleges and Universities. Mr. Eves has served as Chairman of the Public Accounts Committee; he was appointed to the Select Committee on Ontario in Confederation, and served as a member on a number of other legislative committees.

Ernie Eves was born in Windsor in 1946 and attended the University of Toronto and Osgoode Hall Law School. He was called to the Bar in 1972 and was made a Queen's Counsel in January, 1983. Before his election, Mr. Eves was an active member of the business community in Parry Sound and a partner in the local law firm of Green and Eves.

DAVID E.A. GILES has been a professor with the department of Economics, University of Victoria, British Columbia since 1994. He completed his Ph.D. at the University of Canterbury, New Zealand in 1975. Previous positions include professor of Econometrics, University of Canterbury; professor and chair, Department of Econometrics, Monash University, Australia; and head of Research Section, Reserve Bank of

New Zealand. Dr. Giles has published approximately 100 articles in econometric theory and applied econometrics. He is currently the North American Editor of the *Journal of International Trade & Economic Development*, and associate Editor of both the *Journal of Econometrics* and the *Journal of Quantitative Economics*. In addition, he has acted as a consultant for both government and industry in several countries.

HERBERT GRUBEL has been professor of economics at Simon Fraser University since 1971 and has a B.A. from Rutgers University and a Ph.D. in economics from Yale University. He is also the David Somerville Fellow in Taxation and Finance at The Fraser Institute. He has taught full-time at Stanford University, the University of Chicago, and the University of Pennsylvania; he has had temporary appointments at universities in Berlin, Singapore, Cape Town, Nairobi, Oxford, and Canberra. Herbert Grubel was the Reform Party Member of Parliament for Capliano-Howe Sound from 1993 to 1997, serving as the Finance Critic from 1995 to 1997. He has published 16 books and 180 professional articles in economics dealing with international trade and finance and a wide range of economic policy issues.

JOHN MCCALLUM is chief economist with the Royal Bank of Canada, Toronto. He obtained his B.A. from Cambridge University in 1971, a Diplome d'Etudes Superieures from Université de Paris 1 in 1973, and a Ph.D. in Economics from McGill University in 1977. Dr. McCallum is responsible for providing economic analysis and commentary for the Royal Bank and for outside clients and the public. He is the author or co-author of 8 books or monographs as well as many articles. He has written on fiscal and monetary issues, comparative macroeconomic performance of OECD countries, the economic integration of Canada and the United States, and other economic topics.

JANICE MACKINNON is Minister of Economic and Co-operative Development in the Government of Saskatchewan. She received a B.A. from the University of Western Ontario and an M.A. and Ph.D. from Queen's University in Kingston. She taught Canadian-American Relations and Women's History at the University of Saskatchewan and has written two books (one on political culture, the other on women refugees) as well as many articles on the Free Trade Agreement and privatization. Ms. MacKinnon was first elected in October 1991 to represent the Saskatoon Westmount constituency for the Saskatchewan New Democratic Party. On November 1, 1991 she was appointed to Cabinet as Minister of Social Services. She next served as Associate Minister of Finance and Minister Responsible for the Crown Investments Corporation. In January 1993, she was appointed Minister of Finance. During her tenure as Minister of Finance, Saskatchewan was the first senior government in Canada to balance its budget. In June 1995, Ms. MacKinnon was re-elected as the representative for Saskatoon Idylwyld. She was appointed to her current position of Minister of Economic and Cooperative Development and Government House Leader in June 1997.

PRESTON MANNING is Member of Parliament for Calgary Southwest, Leader of the Official Opposition and Leader of the Reform Party of Canada. He received a B.A. in Economics from the University of Alberta. He was first elected to Parliament in 1993 and re-elected in 1997. He was a founder of the Reform Party of Canada, 1987 and its Leader from the same year. He is the official Opposition critic for the President of the Queen's Privy Council for Canada and Intergovernmental Affairs.

TIM REID is the past-President (1989–1998) of the 170,000 member Canadian Chamber of Commerce, Canada's largest and most representative national business association. A Rhodes Scholar, he holds degrees in economics and political science from the Universities of Toronto, Yale, and Oxford, and has also completed the Advanced Management Program at Harvard. He has served as a Commissioner of the Ontario Securities Commission, a deputy secretary of the federal Government's Treasury Board, a Principal Administrator at the OECD in Paris, a Member of Parliament (Ontario Legislature), the Business Co-chair of the Canadian Labour Market and Productivity Centre, and as Dean of the Faculty of Business at Ryerson Polytechnic University, Toronto.

NELSON A. RIIS is the Member of Parliament for Kamloops (New Democratic Party). He has a B.Ed. and an M.A. in geography from the University of British Columbia. Mr. Riis has taught in the public school system and in colleges and universities. He served as an alderman on the Council of the City of Kamloops from 1973 to 1978, was a director of the Thompson-Nicola Regional District, and also an elected trustee for Kamloops School District between from 1978 until his election to Parliament in 1980. Since his election to Parliament, Riis has been the New Democratic Party's spokesperson for Small Business, Regional Expansion, and Finance; he is also Parliamentary House Leader for the Federal Caucus. He currently serves as the spokesperson for Business, Finance and International Financial Institutions and is Chair of the Federal NDP Caucus.

JEFFREY G. RUBIN is Chief Economist and Managing Director of CIBC Wood Gundy, Toronto. Mr. Rubin received a B.A. from the University of Toronto and an M.A. from McGill University. He was senior policy advisor for the Ministry of Finance, Government of Ontario from August 1982 to July 1988.

LUDGER SCHUKNECHT is an economist in the Research and Analysis Division of the World Trade Organization in Geneva. He studied economics in Munich, at George Mason University in Virginia, and in Konstanz, Germany. Specializing in international economics and political economy, he received his Ph.D. from the University of Konstanz with the thesis, *Trade Protection in the European Community* (Harwood Academic Publishers, 1992). He joined the International Monetary Fund (IMF) in 1992 and worked in the African and Fiscal Affairs Departments. His most prominent tasks there included helping to build the fiscal administration in the West Bank and Gaza Strip and the joint work on government reform with Vito Tanzi. He has published articles on a range of issues, including expenditure, policies, political business cycles, EU trade policy, financial services, trade, and electronic commerce. Since January 1997, he has been on leave from the IMF to work at the World Trade Organization.

GERALD SCULLY has been with the School of Management, University of Texas, Richardson, Texas since 1985. In the past 10 years, his focus has been on measuring inefficiency, examining the roles of institutional technology and policy on growth and equity, and other issues in public choice and constitutional political economy. The work on inefficiency is related mainly to the effects of different property rights regimes and issues of vertical integration and multinationality. He has shown that the extent of economic freedom and the rule of law are preconditions for a high rate of economic progress in the Third World. In public choice and constitutional political economy, his main contributions have been on the theory of rent-seeking, the political market for income redistribution, the measurement of the trade-off between equality and efficiency, estimates of the effect of the distribution of rights on economic efficiency and equity, further work on the theory of the rule space and economic growth, and on estimates of growth-maximizing tax rate for the advanced industrial countries.

VITO TANZI is the Director, Fiscal Affairs Department, International Monetary Fund, Washington, DC. Vito Tanzi received his Ph.D. in economics from Harvard University and, before joining the International Monetary Fund in 1974, he was Professor and Chairman, Department of Economics at the American University. He has also been on the faculty of the George Washington University and a consultant for the World

Bank, the United Nations, the Organization of American States, and the Stanford Research Institute. He has published many books including *The Individual Income Tax and Economic Growth* (Johns Hopkins University Press, 1969); *Inflation and the Personal Income Tax* (Cambridge University Press, 1980); *The Underground Economy in the United States and Abroad* (Lexington Press, 1982); *Taxation, Inflation and Interest Rates* (IMF, 1984); *Public Finance in Developing Countries* (Edward Elgar, 1991); and *Taxation in an Integrating World* (Brookings, 1995). He has edited several books, the most recent of which is *Income Distribution and High Quality Growth* (MIT Press, 1998). Dr. Tanzi has written a large number of articles in leading professional journals like the *American Economic Review, The Journal of Political Economy, The Review of Economics and Statistics, The Economic Journal, The Journal of Public Economics.* His major interests are public finance, monetary theory, and macroeconomics. In the period from 1990 to 1994, he was President of the International Institute of Public Finance.

MICHAEL A. WALKER is the Executive Director of The Fraser Institute and has directed its activities since 1974. He is an economist, journalist, broadcaster, consultant, university lecturer, and public speaker. As an economist, he has written or edited 40 books on economic topics. His articles on technical economic subjects have appeared in professional journals. As a journalist, he has written some 600 articles, which have appeared in some 60 newspapers. As a broadcaster, he has written and delivered some 2,000 radio broadcasts on economic topics and appeared on radio and television programs in Canada, the United States, and Latin America. As a consultant, he has provided advice to private groups and governments on five continents. He taught at the University of Western Ontario and Carleton University and was employed at the Bank of Canada and the Federal Department of Finance. He received his Ph.D. at the University of Western Ontario and his B.A. at St. Francis Xavier University.

CONRAD WINN (Ph.D. Wharton) is Chief Executive Officer and founding chairman of Carleton Opinion Marketing and Public Affairs Surveys, Inc. (COMPAS). He is widely known to Canadians as a result of his frequent appearances on television programs like Mike Duffy's *Sunday Edition* and his analysis of trends in *The Financial Post*, the Southam newspaper chain, and elsewhere. Author of five books and many professional articles, he has taught public affairs and communications for almost three decades at undergraduate and doctoral levels in Canada and abroad. Mr. Winn's experience in public affairs, communications, and marketing includes projects with dozens of *Financial Post* 500 corporations, professional bodies, industry groups, non-profit organizations, media, and government departments.

Preface

MICHAEL WALKER

As Canada heads into the next century, the central issue of fiscal policy is what we should do with the surplus. There are three possibilities: increase spending, reduce taxes, or pay off the debt. The purpose of this book is to examine the options and to provide an economic analysis of alternative outcomes. The focus of the book is that the choice that government makes will have direct implications for the comparative size of the government and private sectors. In turn, this outcome has an implication for growth, employment, and future economic stability.

For some, the question of the size of government is purely political and is not amenable to economic analysis. This view is reflected in this volume. For others, the optimal size of government or the optimal tax rate (which is the same thing in a balanced-budget world) is a technical question that can be decided apart from political considerations. The logic of the latter view seems unassailable when considered along the following lines.

On the one hand, every Canadian would agree that a tax rate of 0 percent would be too low. Such a tax rate would provide no revenue to government and, therefore, no government services would be possible. On the other hand, all would agree that a 100 per cent tax rate is too high. Such a rate would imply that there was no private sector at all, since all purchasing decisions would be made by government. Somewhere between the 0 and 100 lies the optimal rate of tax.

In a similar logical fashion, one could eliminate tax rates as low as 10 or 15 percent or as high as 80 or 90 percent. The tax rate between these boundaries that would be best for Canada can be subjected to analysis. The higher the tax rate, the more government services can be provided—though each additional dollar spent on programs beyond a certain level would be expected to produce less and less benefit. Moreover, the higher the tax rate, the greater the disincentives to economic growth and increased employment.

So, while there are many political answers to the question, what should be the size of government, there is an analytical approach that will yield the optimal size of government from an economic point of view. The essays published in this study approach the issue of the optimal size of government from a number of points of departure. In the process, they provide a powerful framework for considering what should be done with the fiscal surplus.

The Fraser Institute was pleased to host the conference that produced this collection of papers and hopes that they will stimulate more cogent discussion of a very important topic. However, it must be noted that the authors have worked independently and the views they express may not conform with those of the members or of the trustees of The Fraser Institute.

How to Use the Fiscal Surplus
What is the Optimal Size
of Government?

Introduction and Summary

HERBERT GRUBEL

When the conference *How to Spend the Fiscal Dividend: What is the Optimal Size of Government?* was planned in the summer of 1997, the Government of Canada was expected to present a balanced budget in the upcoming fiscal year 1998/99 and, if tax rates and spending programs remained unchanged, large annual surpluses in the following years. These expected surpluses have become known as the "fiscal dividend" because they are the return on the "investment" of fiscal restraint practised since 1993.

The government has only three ways in which it can use the fiscal dividend: increased spending, tax cuts, and debt reduction. The papers from the conference (Ottawa, December 3, 1997) published in this book consider the allocation of the expected fiscal dividend among these three competing uses. The well-being of future generations of Canadians depends greatly on the choices the government will make.

History of imbalances and public opinion

Part One provides facts on which the economic and political analysis in the rest of the book should rest.

Canada's fiscal imbalances: history and options for the future

Herbert Grubel shows the changes in spending and revenue that have taken place between 1993 and 1996. He demonstrates that the government eliminated the deficit mainly by means of revenue increases

(75 percent) rather than spending cuts (25 percent). Well over half of the revenue gains came from higher revenues from personal income tax. About $21 billion was cut from program spending but $8 billion of this was off-set by the cost of servicing the growing debt. Further, $8.3 billion of the $21 billion was achieved through a reduction in transfers to other levels of government—a reduction that provincial governments blame for the cuts in spending on health, higher educa-tion, and welfare that they have had to make since 1993.

Professor Grubel also projects recent developments into the future and shows likely annual surpluses of $47 billion by 2003/04. Some simulations of the development of the ratio between debt and GDP and cuts to personal income taxes show that the expected surpluses present rich opportunities for lowering the burden of debt and shrinking the size of government.

What do Canadians think should be done with the fiscal surplus?

Conrad Winn summarizes the results of a public opinion survey that asked Canadians how they thought that the fiscal dividend should be used. The most important result is that debt reduction is preferred by 41 percent, tax cuts by 27 percent, and increased program spending by 32 percent of Canadians.

These basic findings are analyzed in greater depth by considering the demographic characteristics and regional residence of respondents. For example, Albertans by a large margin prefer debt reduction while a clear majority of Canadians in the Atlantic provinces want the govern-ment to use the fiscal dividend to increase spending. Forty-three per-cent of all Canadian men prefer debt reduction while only 37 percent of women do.

The optimal size of government and public well-being

Part Two presents long-term and international perspectives on the op-timal size of government. The findings presented provide powerful ar-guments for using the fiscal dividend for tax cuts and a smaller government. Paying down the debt would produce the same results but at a much slower pace. A smaller government would increase economic efficiency and economic growth without significant sacrifices in indica-tors of social well-being.

Optimal levels of spending and taxation in Canada

In his paper at the conference, Professor Gerald Scully summarized the main findings of his widely discussed studies of the relationship be-tween government spending and economic growth in the United States and New Zealand, drawing parallels to Canada. His theory and econometric methodology were used by Johnny Chao and Herbert Grubel in a formal analysis of Canada's historic experience. They show that between 1928 and the early 1960s increases in government spending and taxation were associated with rising economic growth. However, after 1963, as the size of government exceeded 35 percent of GDP, further increases in government spending were associated with a consistent reduction in economic growth. Their analysis concludes that economic growth in Canada would be increased if spending were lowered from its recent 48 percent of GDP to its historic optimum of 35 percent. Such a reduction in spending and taxation would raise the economic growth rate by 22 percent.

Can small governments secure economic and social well-being?

Ludger Schuknecht reports on work he had undertaken jointly with Vito Tanzi at the IMF. The authors analyzed the relationship between the government spending and economic growth of a number of countries over most of this century. They found that spending at up to about 30 percent of GDP fosters economic growth; thereafter it has a negative effect.

Most importantly, Schuknecht and Tanzi found that, once countries exceed this optimum level of spending, they not only reduced economic growth but also produced no or very minimal gains in social benefits. Countries with high and "moderate" spending levels produce just about the same life expectancy, infant mortality, educational attainment, and environmental qualities. Only for income distribution do the countries with high spending levels have a better record than those with low spending. However, the gains are very modest. In high-spending countries, the poorest 40 percent of households receive 20.1 percent of all income; in countries with moderate and small governments, these shares are 18.7 and 17.3 percent, respectively. According to this evidence, the choice faced by Canada is whether these very modest gains in income equality are worth the reduction in economic growth accompanying the higher government spending needed to bring it about.

The underground economy: minimizing the size of government

Professor David Giles reports on his study of the hidden economy of New Zealand using new data and methodologies. His estimates for Canada suggest that the hidden economy is equal to 15 percent of GDP and implies a loss of $35.5 billion in tax revenue.

Provincial politicians describe recent fiscal history

These chapters describe the recent history of fiscal restraint in Alberta, Saskatchewan, and Ontario.

Lessons from Alberta on fiscal dividends and taxation

Stockwell Day, the Treasurer of Alberta, relates his government's path from very high deficits to large surpluses. He describes the pressures he faced for increased spending once surpluses had developed and how his government's legislated restrictions on spending helped him fend off these demands. Mr. Day also discusses his government's measures to protect against the development of future deficits through prudent, transparent, and binding budgeting procedures.

Balance: fiscal responsibility in Saskatchewan

Janice MacKinnon, Saskatchewan's Minister of Economic and Co-operative Development, reports her government's efforts to restore fiscal balance while it protected social spending and encouraged economic activity through subsidies and tax concessions. Her government's success with these policies suggests that fiscal balance can be restored even while the most important goals of spending are maintained.

Restructuring the government in Ontario

Ernie Eves, the Finance Minister of the Government of Ontario, reports how massive fiscal restraint and tax reductions have been rewarded by substantial growth in economic activity and government revenues, much as historic and broader studies of the economists suggest in the first part of this book.

Discussion of lessons from provincial politicians

This chapter is an edited transcription of a discussion among Mr. Day, Ms. MacKinnon, and Mr. Eves that followed the presentation of their papers at the conference; it includes answers to questions from the audience.

Views of business economists

Three professional economists from the private sector give their views on how the government should spend the fiscal dividend.

Options on the fiscal dividend

John McCallum urges that current spending levels be considered in an historical context. He notes that program spending relative to GDP in 1996 was at its lowest level since 1948. Because of economic growth and a constant nominal debt, by 2006 the ratio of debt to GDP will be lower than it has been since the mid-1960s. He argues that tax cuts should focus on personal income tax rates, which are the highest among the G7 countries, and not on payroll taxes, which are among the lowest—lower even than those in the United States. Tax cuts should be designed to lower the very high marginal tax rates faced by people with low incomes. These high marginal tax rates are the result of increased incomes that lead both to a loss of government benefits and the payment of higher personal taxes. To discourage emigration from Canada of people at the upper end of the income distribution, he also suggests reductions in the high marginal tax rates that they face.

View of the Canadian Chamber of Commerce

Tim Reid, past-President of Canadian Chamber of Commerce presents the views of the Chamber's many members—views determined by an extensive process of consultation before the conference. The Chamber wants the government to "anchor" its gains by paying down the debt and thus reduce the risk that high interest payments will once more result in deficits during future recessions. Mr. Reid urges the government to set targets for debt reduction so it can be held accountable. He also suggests lowering taxes, especially employment insurance premiums. He asks that increased government spending be undertaken only after careful analysis of the costs and benefits for each project—a process that would lead to lower spending relative to GDP in the future.

View of CIBC Wood Gundy

Jeffrey Rubin of CIBC Wood Gundy opposes adamantly the government's practice of playing down its success in fiscal restraint and understating the large surpluses that he sees already in existence or about to appear in the near future. He is pessimistic about the political acceptability of using large surpluses to pay down the debt and urges, instead, that the fiscal dividend be used to reduce personal income taxes, making Canada more competitive with other G7 countries. Mr. Rubin estimates that all of the spending restraints of the last three budgets will quickly be wiped out if the government adheres to its promise to use 50 percent of future surpluses for increased spending.

Discussion of views of business economists

John McCallum of the Royal Bank of Canada believes that the optimal size of government is a political question to be decided at the ballot box and that economic analysis cannot provide the answer. This provoked an extended exchange with Mike Walker during the discussion period, who insisted that economists have important information about the costs and benefits of government spending that voters need to consider before they cast their ballots. This is so even in the case of spending for income redistribution and the inevitable ethical judgements, which should be made rationally in the light of information about the reductions in economic growth that accompany policies of income redistribution.

Views of the federal political parties

Preston Manning, Nelson Riis and Jean Charest explain the positions of three major political parties. The Liberals had been invited but failed to send a speaker.

View of the Reform Party

Preston Manning expresses interest in the economic analysis of optimal spending levels but offers, instead, a pragmatic formula for the use of the fiscal dividend: spending should increase at the rate of 6 percent annually to keep up with inflation, income, and population growth; remaining surpluses should be divided equally between tax relief and debt reduction.

View of the New Democratic Party

Nelson Riis finds the Liberal formula for distribution of the fiscal dividend acceptable: 50 percent of the surplus is to be used for increases in spending, 25 percent for debt reduction and 25 percent for tax relief. He identifies students with large debts, Medicare, impoverished children, and the unemployed as the most important recipients of increased spending.

Views of the Progressive Conservative Party

Jean Charest disputes the existence of a fiscal dividend on the grounds that any surpluses are the result of excessively high unemployment-insurance premiums, which have resulted in an unnecessarily large surplus in the EI account administered by the government. M. Charest suggests that income taxes be cut immediately to increase productivity and government revenues, and to reduce incentives for the brain drain.

Conclusion

In my view, one of the most important conclusions which emerged from the conference is as follows. Canada's fiscal performance has been and in the future will strongly be influenced by automatic revenue growth due to the broadening of the tax base and higher taxes paid on a constant real income base. This latter phenomenon is very important. It is due to the "bracket creep," which results in higher income-tax payments as inflation erodes the real value of personal exemptions and forces the payment of higher marginal income-tax rates.

Revenue growth due to bracket creep sends the wrong signals to politicians. Without having to face the wrath of the electorate over explicit tax hikes, they discover fiscal surpluses available for increased spending. If they use future surpluses for this purpose, the size of government in the economy will continue to grow. The recent period of fiscal restraint will have eliminated the deficit and lowered the ratio of debt to GDP. But the inefficiencies and reduced economic growth due to a larger government will end up being greater than they were before the fiscal crisis of the last decade.

These developments can be avoided only by lowering tax rates and paying down the debt. In addition, the indexing of personal exemptions and brackets in the personal income tax should be fully restored. If politicians in future governments want to court the favour of voters through higher spending, they should be forced to face these same voters with explicit tax increases to pay for the increases.

The History of Fiscal Imbalances and Public Opinion

Canada's Fiscal Imbalances

History and Options for the Future

Herbert G. Grubel

The rational discussion of the fiscal options available to Canada in the upcoming years should be based on shared knowledge about current conditions, historic developments, and the likely effects of adopting alternative policies. This chapter presents, first, a series of graphs (figures 1–9) that summarize some facts about Canada's recent fiscal history and how the deficit was eliminated. A second series of graphs (figures 10–13) shows projections of future revenues, spending levels, and surpluses. Finally, a third series of graphs (figures 14–18) shows debt and spending programs in relation to national income in an historic context. Simulations of the use of the future surpluses put the resultant future ratios into an historic perspective.

Series 1: How the deficit was eliminated

The graphs in this section show first the most highly aggregate data on spending and revenues. These data are then broken down into main components and these, in turn, are broken down to reveal increasing details. All spending and revenue estimates for the period 1993/94 through 1998/99 are from successive issues of the *Budget Plan* released annually by the Government when each year's budget is presented to parliament. The figures for 1996/97 given in the *1997 Budget Plan* were corrected according to *The Economic and Fiscal Update* published in October 1997. The years 1997/98 and 1998/99 equal these updated figures plus the changes indicated in the *1997 Budget Plan*.

Comment on figure 1: The trend in imbalances between 1993/94 and 1998/99 is impressive by historic and international standards. The deficit of $40 billion in 1993/94 turned into a surplus of $4.1 billion in 1998/99.

Comment on figure 2: The deficit was eliminated predominantly through revenue increases of $33.4 billion (equal to 72.5 percent) while the net decrease in spending was only $12.7 billion (equal to 27.5 percent of the original deficit).

Comment on figure 3: The increased revenues were obtained mainly through increased collection of personal income tax (56.9 percent), corporate income tax (26.7 percent) and excise taxes (GST) and duties (12.2 percent).

Comment on figure 4: The net decrease in spending is composed of reduced program spending of $20.7 billion and an increase of $8 billion for servicing the debt created by the deficits in the early years.

Comment on figure 5: Note that the increase in the size of the debt = $111.1 billion; increase in interest paid = $8.0 billion; interest rate on increased debt = 7.2%.

Comment on figure 6: Transfers to persons dropped only $1.2 billion (5.7 percent of the total). The reduction of $20.7 billion in program spending was achieved mainly through cuts in direct program spending of $11.2 billion and cuts in transfers to other levels of government of $8.3 billion. The latter cut, "downloading" the deficit on provincial governments, represents 40.1 percent of all reductions in program spending.

Comment on figure 7: The reduction in net transfers to persons of $1.2 billion was the result of a reduction in payments of unemployment insurance benefits of $4.2 billion and an *increase* in transfers to the elderly of $3 billion.

Comment on figure 8: The reductions in transfers to other levels of government were accomplished primarily through cuts in Canadian health and social transfers of $6.9 billion (83.1 percent of total) and cuts of only $1.4 billion (16.9 percent) in other transfers.

Comment on figure 9: Subsidies and transfers to Indians and Inuit *increased* by $1.1 billion, spending on defence was cut by $1.4 billion, and all the other program spending absorbed the bulk of the cuts of $11 billion.

Figure 1: Federal Spending Imbalances

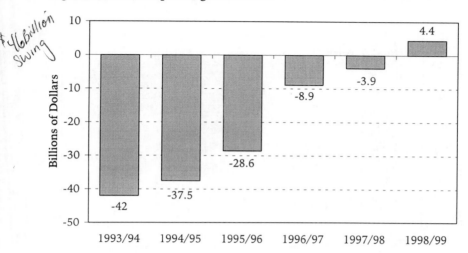

$46 Billion Swing

Figure 2: Sources of Deficit Elimination

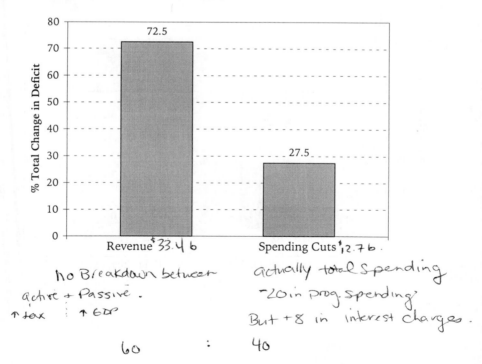

Revenue $33.4 b

no Breakdown between active + Passive.
↑ tax : ↑ GDP

60

Spending Cuts $12.7 b.

actually total Spending
-20 in prog. spending
But +8 in interest charges.

40

Figure 3: Sources of Increased Revenue (% of $33.4 billion)

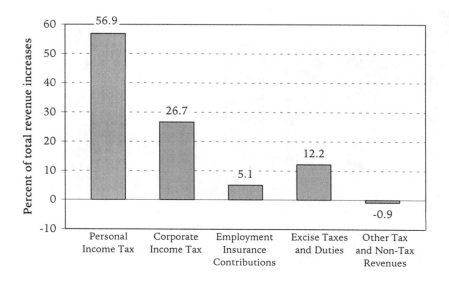

Figure 4: Sources of Changed Spending

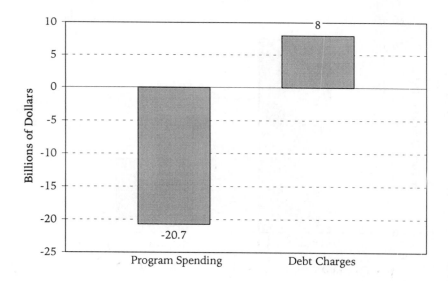

Figure 5: Some Facts about Interest on Debt

Fiscal Years	1993/ 1994	1994/ 1995	1995/ 1996	1996/ 1997	1997/ 1998	1998/ 1999
Interest paid ($billion)	38.0	42.0	46.9	45.5	46.0	46.5
Size of debt ($billion)	508.2	545.7	574.3	593.3	610.3	619.3
Interest rate on debt (interest paid/size of debt)	7.5	7.7	8.2	7.7	7.5	7.4

$$\text{TOTAL interest payments} = \left(\frac{\text{Int}}{\text{Rate}}\right) \times (\text{P·Debt})$$

between 93/94 → 98/99 $\quad (-1.3\%) \times (+21.9\%)$

$+22\% \quad\uparrow\; = \atop{7.5\% - 7.4\%} \quad (508 - 619)$

Figure 6: Sources of Change in Program Spending

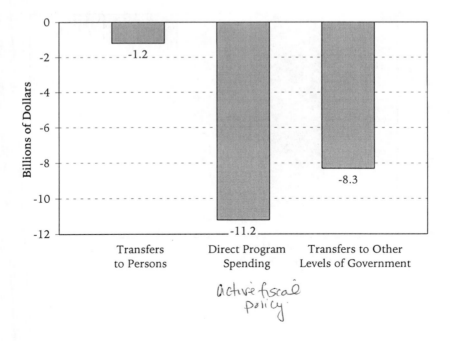

active fiscal policy

Figure 7: Changes in Transfers to Persons

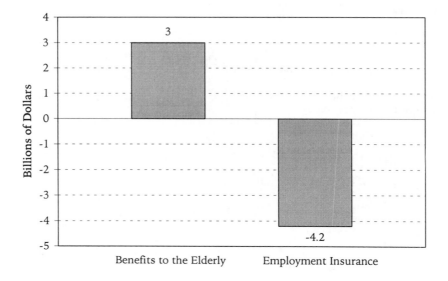

Figure 8: Transfers to Other Levels of Government

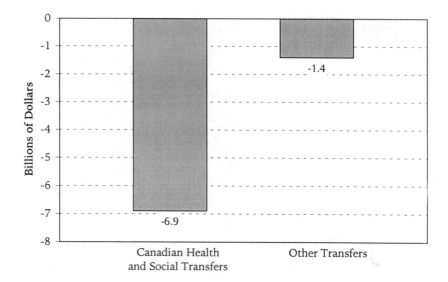

Figure 9: Changes in Direct Program Spending

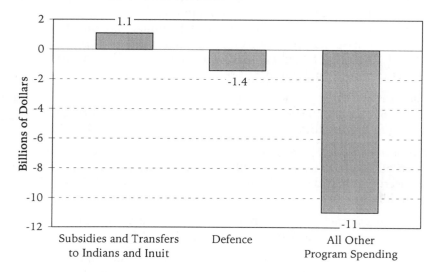

Series 2: Projections of revenue and spending

My projections for the five years following 1998/99 are based on the simple assumption that the next five years will bring more or less the same revenue growth as did the preceding five years; *i.e.*, that there will be some years with good economic conditions and some that are marred by slower growth because of a cyclical downturn or a shock like that coming from the Mexican crisis in 1994. It seems reasonable to expect, therefore, that revenues from personal income tax will continue to grow at an annual average rate of 6.5 percent.

The annual rate of increase in revenue from corporate income tax was even higher than that from the personal income tax, given the low levels in 1992/93 after the recession. I assumed, therefore, that the growth rate of income from corporate income tax over the next five years will only be 4.6 percent annually, the rate for the years 1995 through 1998. Revenue from employment insurance premiums grew at 1.75 percent and that from excise taxes and duties at 2.9 percent annually during the base period. I assumed that these rates will be repeated for the following five years.

I assumed that discretionary spending will remain fixed at its 1998/99 levels for all categories except the cost of servicing the debt and providing benefits to the elderly. The cost of servicing the debt is reduced every year by the interest saved through the use of annual surpluses to lower the debt; I assumed an interest rate of 8 percent. Benefits to the elderly are assumed to rise at an annual rate of 3.3 percent; during the base period, they rose 2.8 percent per year between 1993/94 and 1998/99. I added one-half of a percentage point to this rate to reflect the increasing number of retirees in Canada.

Comment on figure 10: Assuming broadly that revenue growth during the five years after 1998/99 will be the same as it was during the preceding five years, total revenues will be $187 billion in 2003/04.

Comment on figure 11: Assuming broadly that all spending programs remain unchanged at their 1998/99 level and that interest payments are reduced through debt retirement, total spending in 2003/04 will be $140 billion.

Comment on figure 12: The projected revenue and spending developments result in a $46.7 billion surplus in 2003/04.

Comment on figure 13: The graph shows the annual spending imbalances, actual and projected. They are equal to the difference between revenues and spending shown in figure 12.

Figure 10: Actual and Projected Revenue

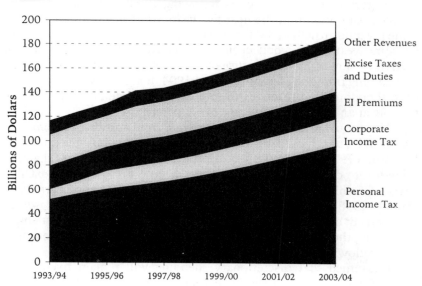

Figure 11: Actual (1993 –1998) and Projected Spending

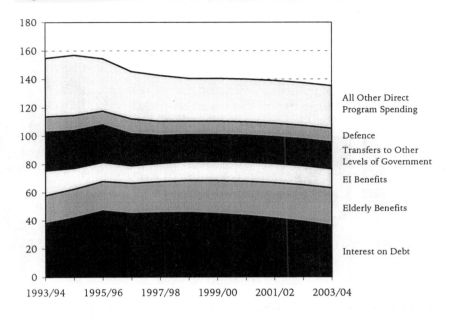

Figure 12: Total Revenues and Spending

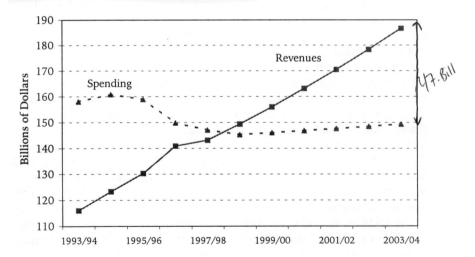

Figure 13: Federal Spending Imbalances

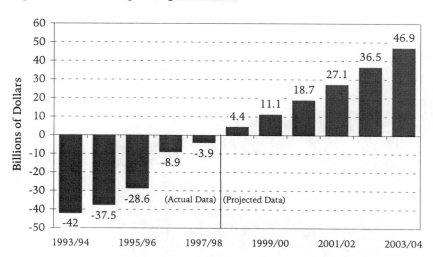

Series 3: Simulated effects of policy measures

The final section of this paper presents the ratio of the federal gross debt to GDP in historic perspective from 1970 to 1997. For the following years to 2003/04, the ratio is simulated assuming that GDP will grow at 2.5 percent per year and that none, all, or one-half of the projected surpluses are used to reduce the existing debt.

A second simulation is designed to provide insights into the size of some major categories of government spending relative to the size of the economy. For this purpose, I would have liked to use the spending categories found in recent Budgets. Unfortunately, Statistics Canada has readily available only spending in categories that seem to have their origin in Musgrave's well-known taxonomy: Federal Expenditures on Goods and Services (including investment), Transfers to Persons, and Transfers to Other Levels of Government. I plotted the ratios of spending in these three categories relative to GDP for the years 1970 to 1996. For the following years to 2003/04, I assumed that spending was frozen at the 1996 levels and that GDP was growing at an 2.5 percent annually.

The final simulation involves the ratio of revenue from personal income tax to GDP since 1970 and projected into the future on the assumption that none, all, or one-half of all surpluses are applied to the reduction of tax rates.

Comment on figure 14: The debt to GDP ratio has risen steadily and steeply after 1981. This trend has peaked in 1996. Declines in the ratio have taken place since then and will continue at rates dependent upon the government's use of the fiscal surplus.

Comment on figure 15: If the total amounts of the budget surpluses are applied to debt reduction and the economy grows at 2.5 percent annually, the ratio of debt to GDP will fall quickly. In 2003/04, it will be 51 percent, equal to that of the mid-1980s.

Comment on figure 16: If expenditures on goods and services are kept at the 1996 levels and the economy grows at 2.5 percent annually, in 2003/ 04 they will be 3.2 percent of GDP, roughly half of their level in 1970.

Comment on figure 17: If transfers to persons are kept at their 1996 levels and the economy grows at 2.5 percent annually, in 2003/04 they will reach 1989 levels and transfers to other levels of government in 2003/04 will be 25 percent below their peak in 1970.

Comment on figure 18: If all fiscal surpluses were applied to reductions in the income tax, income tax receipts as a percent of GDP would drop quickly and substantially to 1.5 percent of GDP.

Figure 14: Ratio of Debt to GDP from 1970 to 2003 Combined federal and Provincial

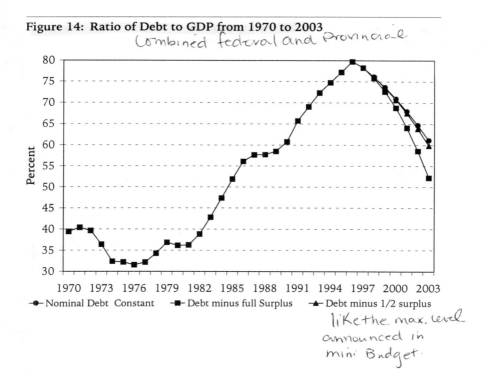

like the max. level announced in mini Budget.

Figure 15: Ratio of Debt to GDP, details

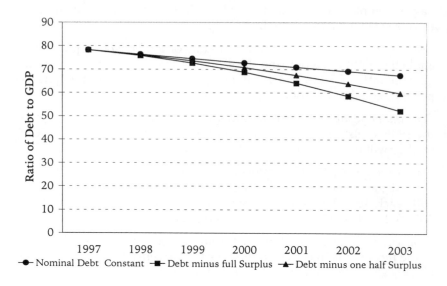

Figure 16: Ratio of Government Expenditure on Goods and Services to GDP

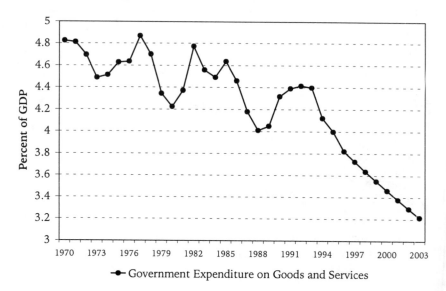

Figure 17: Ratios of Transfers to GDP

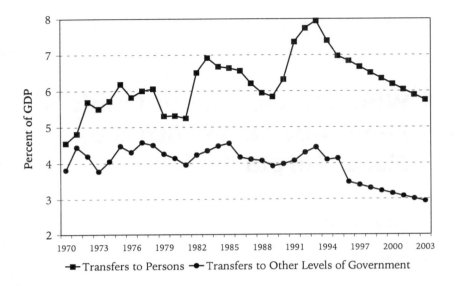

Figure 18: Ratio of Revenue from Personal Income Tax to GDP

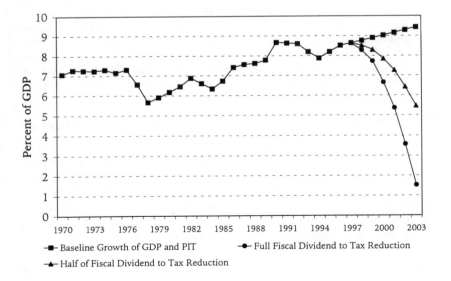

What Do Canadians Think Should Be Done with the Fiscal Surplus?

CONRAD WINN

Editor's Note: At the conference, How to Spend the Fiscal Dividend: What is the Optimal Size of Government? *(Ottawa, December 3, 1997), Conrad Winn presented an interesting and highly informative paper that contained the broad, general results of a survey that Southam News had commissioned from his firm Carleton Opinion Marketing and Public Affairs Surveys, Inc. (COMPAS). This survey probed the attitudes of Canadians on a range of fiscal policy issues. Unfortunately, Dr. Winn could not present precise details of the survey during his presentation because it was to be released officially only a few days later. This chapter draws on the detailed findings published by COMPAS at its Internet website (www.compas.ca) after the Conference. Dr Winn edited and approved the text.*

Pay Down the Debt, Increase Spending, or Reduce Taxes?

The most fundamental finding of the survey was that, on average, Canadians want 41 percent of the surplus to be used for paying down the debt, 27 percent to be used for reducing taxes, and 32 percent to be used for increased program spending (figure 1). This key finding emerges from a very large and detailed nation-wide survey conducted for Southam News and used by the organization to publish a series of interpretive news reports. The core survey of $n = 1700$ was conducted in late November 1997 with sufficient oversamples in Alberta and British Columbia to allow inter-provincial comparisons there as well as in Ontario and Quebec. (For details on sampling issues as well as on the

Figure 1: Average percentages of the surplus to go to debt, tax cut, and spending—responses from the first time this question was asked

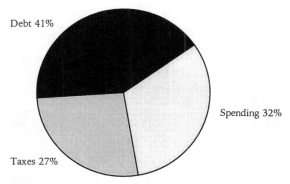

Debt 41%

Spending 32%

Taxes 27%

Source: COMPAS for Southam News, Winter, 1997/8.

precursor mini-surveys that were conducted to test the impact of wording changes, see the archives in www.compas.ca.)

Reasons for emphasis on paying down the debt

When Canadians were asked why paying down the debt should be a priority, they gave the following replies (the percentage of respondents is given in parenthesis).

(1) The debt should be reduced so that future governments could spend the savings from reduced interest payments to lower taxes or on program spending (89 percent).

(2) Young people should not be saddled with a financial burden that they did not create themselves (87 percent).

(3) The debt should be reduced because, once the large baby-boom generation retires from the workforce, there will not be enough younger people to pay taxes and the debt (81 percent).

There is a wide-spread consensus about the importance of debt repayment and what proportion of the surplus should go to the debt. Irrespective of province, age and most other demographic characteristics, Canadians are largely of one mind.

Regional and income differences

Figure 2 shows that Albertans are more interested in debt reduction and much less in tax cuts and spending increases than are the residents of the Atlantic provinces. However, the results from these two regions

Figure 2: Average percentages of the surplus to go to debt, tax cut, and spending—responses from Canada, Alberta, and the Atlantic region

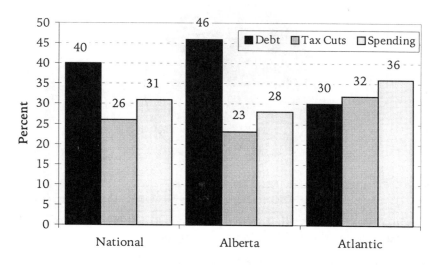

Source: COMPAS for Southam News, Winter, 1997/8.

are not very much different from those for the country as a whole and accurately reflect a broad Canadian consensus on the question of the use of future fiscal surpluses.

Depending on their age, people will be affected in radically different ways by the speed with which the debt is repaid. The youngest would benefit most and the oldest least from an early retirement of the debt. Nevertheless, survey responses not shown here indicate that there are no differences in the share of the fiscal surplus that Canadians of all ages say should be devoted to debt reduction.

There are, however, some significant differences among the views expressed by Canadians with different levels of income regarding the use of the fiscal surplus: the higher the income of the respondents, the higher the proportion of the surplus they want to go to debt reduction and the lower the proportion they want to go to spending increases (figure 3).

Strong desire for faster debt repayment

The issue of the speed with which the debt is repaid was raised by informing respondents that in 1997 the debt was equal to 73 percent of national production. They were then asked their views about the merit of the federal government's announced plan of cutting the its debt to

Figure 3: Average percentages of the surplus to go to repayment of the debt or spending—responses from different household income groups

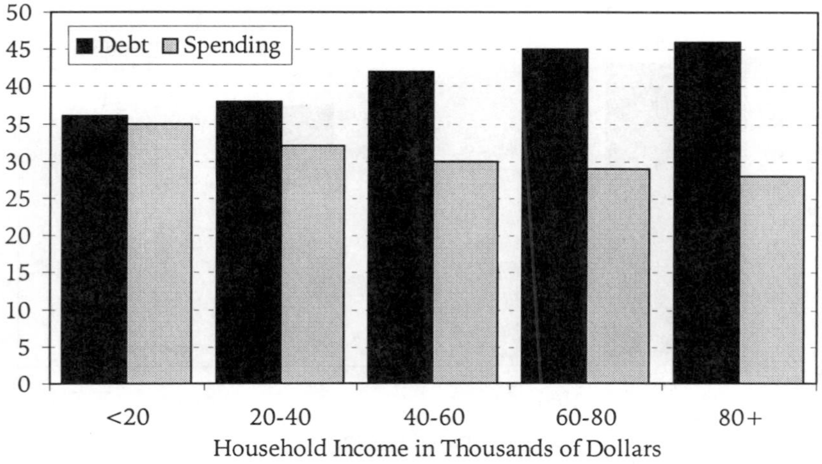

Household Income in Thousands of Dollars

Source: COMPAS for Southam News, Winter, 1997/8.

60 percent in 10 years. In response, 5 percent said that the government plan is much too fast, 31 percent that it was somewhat too fast, 37 percent that it was somewhat too slow, and 12 percent that it was much too slow. The remaining 15 percent feel that this plan is about right.

Disagreement between men and women

It is well know that women increasingly vote for parties of the left and men increasingly for parties of the right. The survey showed that there are also significant differences between their opinions about the use of the future fiscal surplus. Figure 4 shows women prefer spending over debt reduction by a margin of 6 percentage points.

Conclusions

There is a strong consensus among Canadians about the importance of debt repayment. Canadians want a higher proportion of the surplus to go to debt repayment than to tax cuts and spending. Canadians also want a rate of debt repayment faster than that envisaged by the government in 1997. The commitment to debt repayment is rooted deeply in Canadians' sense of propriety and common sense. However, Canadians are not totally united in their concern about debt. For example, men are more enthusiastic about debt repayment than women, Albertans more than Atlantic Canadians, and high income earners more than low income earners.

Figure 4: Average percentages of the surplus to go to debt, tax cut, and spending—men versus women

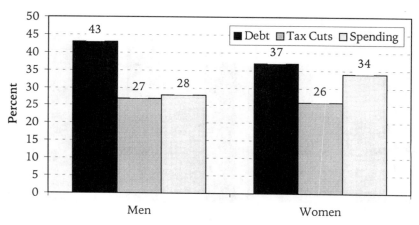

Source: COMPAS for Southam News, Winter, 1997/8.

It is interesting to note that, after a series of questions about the debt, respondents were asked how well informed they felt they had been about the facts before the interview had taken place. About three-fifths felt that they had had a good or very good awareness of debt issues before the interview.

Views on taxation

The survey results presented in the preceding section indicated that Canadians give a lower priority to tax cuts than to increased program spending and especially to debt repayment. From this fact it might be concluded that Canadians are acquiescent about taxes. But such an inference would be wrong.

The survey asked Canadians to evaluate the merit of a number of reasons to cut taxes. The results are shown in figure 5. These results suggest that Canadians are more angry about taxes than they are willing to reveal when asked directly. If this is true, Canadians may well under-report how much of the surplus they would like to be allocated to tax reduction.

Regional and income differences

There are some interesting differences in the degree to which Canadians from different regions of the country believe that taxes are too high (see figure 6).

Figure 5: How the public feels about various reasons to cut taxes—percent who agree "a lot" rather than "somewhat," "not really," or "not at all"

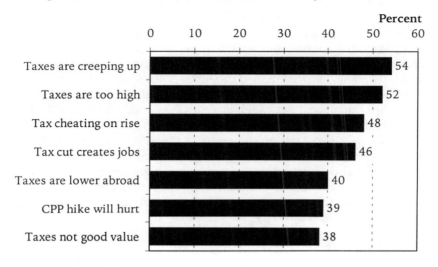

Source: COMPAS for Southam News, Winter, 1997/8.

Figure 6: More easterners than Albertans see taxes as too high—percent "agreeing a lot" that taxes are too high)

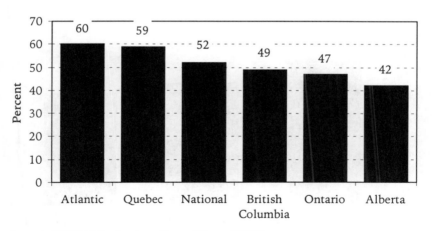

Source: COMPAS for Southam News, Winter, 1997/8.

It is noteworthy that these replies are not well correlated with the present levels of taxation in the regions. Both British Columbia and Ontario, after a period under NDP provincial governments, have very high marginal tax rates. The top British Columbia marginal rate of 55 percent is the highest in Canada. On the other hand, there is an interesting and strong negative correlation between per-capita income levels and the greatest concern over the high levels of taxes. Canadians living in regions like the Atlantic provinces, with the lowest income levels per capita, want taxes lowered the most while those living in provinces with the highest per-capita incomes (Ontario, Alberta and British Columbia) want them lowered much less.

In Canada, taxes rise on average with the level of income. Marginal and average tax rates also are higher, the higher the level of income. One would therefore expect concern over high taxes to be greater among those with college and university education than those with a high school or less. The survey results shown in figure 7 indicate that this is not so. These survey results are a puzzle.

Taxing the rich and corporations?

During the last few decades, surveys revealed that a substantial majority of Canadians accept the principles that it is fine to "tax the rich" and impose higher taxes on corporations. In this survey, their answers were different. Only 60 percent agreed with the statement: "We should continue to pay the present level of taxes because a lot of high-income people can afford to pay a lot more in taxes."

**Figure 7: The educated seem less worried about taxes—
percent "agreeing a lot" that taxes are too high**

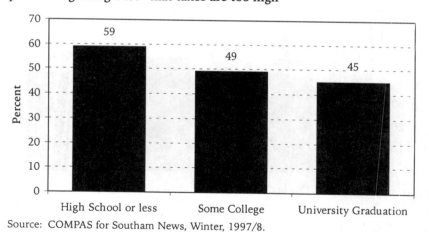

Source: COMPAS for Southam News, Winter, 1997/8.

Clear majorities of the public agreed with a series of reasons that are often given for *lowering* corporate taxes. The wording of the question and response distribution (in parentheses) are as follows.

Another issue is corporation tax, the income taxes businesses pay. Please tell me how you feel about each of the following reasons why corporation taxes should be reduced. First of all, high corporation taxes are a bad idea because:

(1) High corporate taxes drive too many businesses out of the country (total percent agreeing a lot or somewhat—67 percent; agree a lot—31 percent)

(2) Companies will figure out how to pay their taxes in another country that has lower taxes (total percent agreeing a lot or somewhat—67 percent; agree a lot—28 percent)

(3) Corporations are owned by millions of people saving for retirement through their pension plans or RRSPs (total percent agreeing a lot or somewhat—52 percent; agree a lot—16 percent).

Respondents were also asked "what percent of [a tax] cut ... out of a 100 ... should be personal and what percent corporate." They suggested that 35 percent of any tax reduction be given to corporations and 65 percent to individuals. Given the history of Canadians' attitude towards the taxation of corporations, these results are quite extraordinary.

A breakdown of survey respondents on the issue of taxation by age and income also are puzzling. It is generally true that Canadians with higher incomes have larger total retirement investments and shares of these investments in corporate equities than do those with less income. For this reason, one would expect older Canadians and those with higher incomes to be more sympathetic to corporations than younger Canadians with lower incomes. The survey results show this expectation to be false (see figures 8 and 9).

Allocating the tax cuts

What groups of Canadians should be given the largest tax cuts? Figure 10 shows the results of the survey on this issue. These results suggest that Canadians want tax policy to be made on the basis of ethical values. They would give the largest tax reductions to the working poor with children, to families where one parent is at home and others considered to have low incomes and needs based on socially desirable criteria. Taxation is not seen as an instrument to be used by government to stimulate the economy or to advance the country's interests in a

Figure 8: The poor are more sympathetic to corporations than the rich—average percentage of tax cuts to go to corporations)

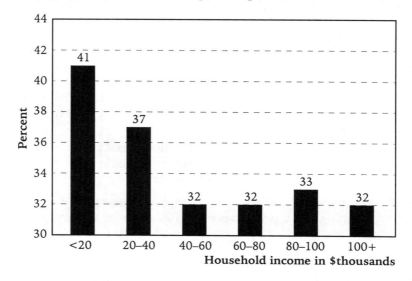

Source: COMPAS for Southam News, Winter, 1997/8.

Figure 9: The young are more sympathetic to corporations than the old—average percentage of tax cuts to go to corporations)

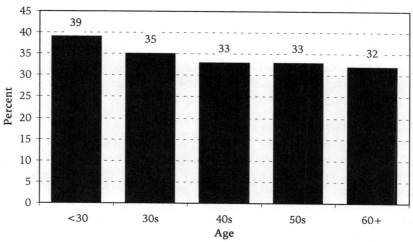

Source: COMPAS for Southam News, Winter, 1997/8.

Figure 10: Types of people whose tax burdens should be reduced—percent agreeing "a lot" rather than "somewhat," "not really," or "not at all."

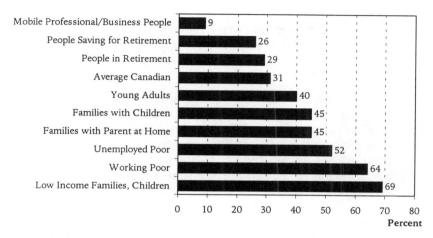

Source: COMPAS for Southam News, Winter, 1997/8.

global marketplace. In particular, Canadians appear not be concerned about the possibility that mobile professionals and business people might relocate to foreign jurisdictions where taxes are lower. On all of the issues presented in Figure 10, there are no significant differences in response according to the respondents' education, income, region, or other demographic attributes.

Views on tax reform

The survey also asked broader questions about changes to the existing system of taxation. These tax reforms have several aspects.

Types of tax cuts

The following issues were raised (response distributions are given in parentheses).

(1) "Employment insurance premiums should be cut to encourage business to hire more people." (total agreement—68 percent; agree a lot—27 percent)

(2) "Personal income taxes should be cut for most middle income earners (*e.g.* people earning about $60,000) because they now have to pay the same percentage of tax as the rich on any extra income they earn." (total agreement—75 percent; agree a lot—38 percent)

(3) "Personal income taxes should be cut for those earning $60,000 or more because federal governments have not kept their promise that the tax increases on these people would only be temporary." (total agreement—53 percent; agree a lot—22 percent)

(4) "As you know, people have to start to pay taxes when they have income of around $6,500. This amount should be increased because it has not changed in 10 years." (total agreement—79 percent; agree a lot—54 percent)

The public consensus for raising the basic exemption, cutting middle-income earners' marginal tax rate, and cutting employment insurance premiums is very strong. A breakdown of these results shows that Canadians support these possibilities irrespective of region, age, gender, education, or income. The most important exception to this finding came from Quebecois, who are more enthusiastic about all tax cuts than Canadians as a whole.

Another intriguing variation involves the income of respondents (see figure 11). These results are noteworthy because in surveys, as well as politics, people have a tendency to avoid the appearance that

Figure 11: Mid-income tax cuts: most agree and mid-earners especially enthusiastic—percent agreeing "a lot" with mid-income tax cut)

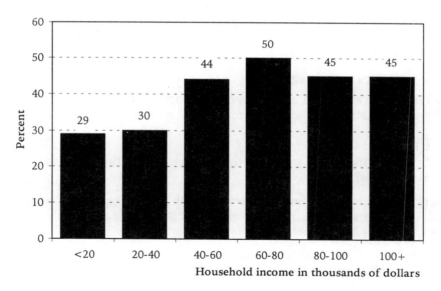

Source: COMPAS for Southam News, Winter, 1997/8.

they want policies to serve their self-interest. This tendency does not hold with respect to tax reductions for middle-income earners. They strongly support such benefits for themselves.

Widespread desire for lowering all taxes

Canada has many types of taxes, of which the GST is one of the most widely discussed. Figure 12 shows the proportion of a given fiscal surplus that respondents thought should go to the reduction of different types of taxes. The largest and almost equally desired reductions are in the income and GST taxes. The GST appears to be of less concern to Canadians than one might have expected from past political discussions. Total revenues raised through employment taxes and the importance of Retirement Savings Plans are minor relative to those involved in personal and corporate income taxation and the GST. Therefore, the desire to have changes made to these systems comes as somewhat of a surprise. Possibly respondents showed their concern over the widely publicized job-killing effects of employment taxes.

The demographic break-down of responses to the questions about the type of taxes that should be cut revealed that younger people show more interest than older people in the reduction of taxes on private Retirement Savings Plans. This may be considered a reflection of the concern of younger people about the ability of the public pension system, the CPP, and Seniors Benefit Plan to meet their needs when they are retired.

Figure 12: Public want surplus to help lower all taxes—proportion of surplus used to cut selective taxes

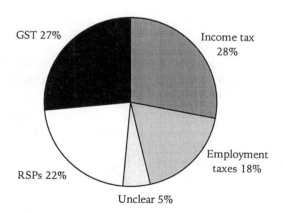

Source: COMPAS for Southam News, Winter, 1997/8.

About marginal tax rates

The survey asked about marginal tax rates, which are considered important by many because of their possible effects on work efforts and investment incentives. To set the stage for questions on this issue, interviewers provided the following introduction:

> One issue in taxation policy is deciding what is a high income. As you know, the government decides what is high income and charges people above this level a higher percentage of their income as tax. This is called "the marginal tax rate." In practice, the marginal tax rate jumps twice—it goes up quite a bit when people earn $30,000 a year and goes up a little bit more when people earn about $60,000 a year. In your view, when should the first tax increase take place? How much should people be earning before they get a big jump in their tax bill? At what income level should the second tax increase take place? That is, how much should a person be making before they're charged at a higher marginal tax rate?

The response to these questions is found in figure 13. It is clear that the public wants the first increase in the marginal tax rate to be applied to people earning $51,000 a year and the second to those earning $80,000 a year. There is a substantial nation-wide consensus on this issue with minor variations associated with the prosperity of the province or region:

(1) Atlantic Canadians suggest slightly lower transition points— $46,000 instead of the nation-wide figure of $51,000 and $75,000 instead of $80,000.

(2) Quebecois also suggest slightly lower transition points—$48,000 and $74,000.

(3) British Columbians offer slightly higher transition points than the national average—$56,000 instead of the nation-wide figure of $51,000 and $90,000 instead of $80,000.

The response to this question hardly varies at all according to respondents' income levels. Respondents from all income strata suggested that the first marginal tax increase should take place in the very tight range of $48,000 to $51,000. The second increase in the marginal rate was given in the range of $76,000 to $83,000 by most respondents. The exception occurred among respondents from households with $100,000 or more in income. This category of very high income earners wants the second increase in marginal tax to take effect at $94,000.

Figure 13: Actual and desired marginal rates of income tax—at what income level should the first and second increases be applied?

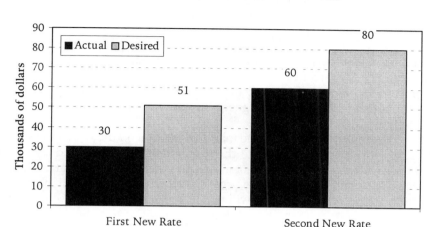

Source: COMPAS for Southam News, Winter, 1997/8.

Marginal rates and the desire to work

Do high marginal tax rates discourage work? To explore this issue, the survey asked Canadians presently working part-time or full-time to describe their willingness to accept extra work under varying marginal tax rates. The survey used the following questions:

> Suppose someone other than your principal employer or your principal source of work offered you two days of extra work each week for 10 weeks, where you would be paid overtime wages at your normal rate of pay. Suppose you took home 50 percent of this because the other 50 percent went to the federal and provincial governments as tax. Would you definitely, probably, probably not or definitely not accept the extra work?

> Suppose you got to keep 70 percent and 30 percent went to the federal and provincial governments as tax. Would you definitely, probably, probably not, or definitely not accept the extra work?

> Suppose you got to keep 90 percent and 10 percent went to the federal and provincial governments as tax. Would you definitely, probably, probably not, or definitely not accept the extra work?

If the respondent was not in the paid workforce but cohabiting with someone who was, COMPAS interviewers asked the respondent whether he or she would encourage their spouse to accept the extra work under these same marginal tax-rate scenarios. The results of these questions are presented in figure 14.

The results show that marginal tax rates have quite a dramatic effect on Canadians' willingness to work. If the marginal rate is dropped to 30 percent from 50 percent, the willingness to work goes up from 28 percent to 77 percent. A further drop of the marginal rate to 10 percent increases willingness to work further but by only a relatively small margin.

The impact of changing the marginal tax rate on the willingness to work is essentially unrelated to the respondent's income or education but has a strong regional character. At a 50 percent marginal rate, Quebecois are much less willing to accept extra work than Canadians as a whole: 11 percent, definitely willing; 17 percent, probably willing; 42 percent, definitely unwilling. This compares with the national averages: 15 percent, definitely willing; 26 percent, probably willing; 32 percent, definitely unwilling. At a 30 percent marginal tax rate, the interest of the Quebecois in work jumps so dramatically that it almost matches the national average: 30 percent definitely willing to work compared to 28 percent nationally; 42 percent probably willing compared to 49 percent; and 16 percent definitely not willing compared to 11 percent.

Figure 14: Percent willing to work weekends under various marginal tax-rate scenarios

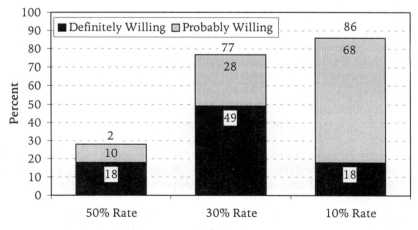

Source: COMPAS for Southam News, Winter, 1997/8.

Government spending and social programs

The survey asked Canadians about the role of government spending and the provision of social programs. The first set of questions (response distributions are given in parentheses) was introduced: "People give different reasons for being thrifty and not spending more money. How do you feel about each of the following ideas?"

(1) "If governments spend less money, they will learn to spend smarter." (agree a lot—41 percent; somewhat—31 percent; total agreement—72 percent)

(2) "If Canadians want better government programs, we should have user fees, not higher taxes." (agree a lot—31 percent; somewhat—38 percent; total agreement—69 percent)

(3) "If governments spend less, Canadians will learn how to do more for themselves." (agree a lot—27 percent; somewhat—35 percent; total agreement—62 percent)

The second set of questions was introduced: "At this point I am going to read you a list of principles that could guide spending. Please tell me how you feel about each principle."

(1) "Expenditures should be closely monitored so that people getting money actually do what they get the money for." (agree a lot—75 percent; somewhat—19 percent; total agreement—95 percent)

(2) "Expenditures should be closely monitored by independent, non-governmental groups so that these programs actually achieve what they are supposed to and don't make things worse." (agree a lot—63 percent; somewhat—27 percent; total agreement—90 percent)

(3) "People should get welfare or other social support for short, fixed periods of time, not forever." (agree a lot—61 percent; somewhat—24 percent; total agreement—85 percent)

(4) "Among people with low incomes, people who work should be helped more than people who don't." (agree a lot—31 percent; somewhat—31 percent; total agreement—62 percent)

(5) "Anyone receiving a government service should have to pay something, even if the user fee were a small one." (agree a lot—35 percent; somewhat—33 percent; total agreement—67 percent)

The third set of questions was designed to uncover Canadians' commitment to liberal principles of redistribution. Respondents were asked to express their agreement with the following statements.

(1) "Among people who work, those with low incomes should be helped more than people with medium incomes." (agree a lot—33 percent; somewhat—42 percent; total agreement—76 percent)

(2) "Children and their parents should be helped more than adults without children." (agree a lot—37 percent; somewhat—34 percent; total agreement—71 percent)

The responses in this section reveal an interesting new development. On the one hand, the views on the last two statements show continued strong support for liberal principles of redistribution. On the other hand, there was even stronger support for the monitoring of social programs and of the behaviour of recipients. It is interesting to note that on all of these issues there exists a strong national consensus and there are no significant differences in responses according to their age, gender, education, and income.

However, Quebecois stand out slightly from other Canadians as a result of their greater preference for charity. In Quebec, 52 percent agree a lot that low-income earners should get priority attention over middle-income earners. In all of Canada, only 33 percent agree with this principle. Quebecois also differ with other Canadians about user fees for government services: 44 percent agree a lot with this principle while only 35 percent of all Canadians and 24 percent of those living in Atlantic Canada agree a lot with this principle.

Paradoxically, the public is especially enthusiastic about spending in those regions, notably Quebec and Atlantic Canada, where antagonism to taxation is especially high.

How to spend money

This section deals with questions in the survey concerning the way in which government should spend that share of the fiscal surplus not going to the reduction of the debt and taxes.

Figure 15 reveals clearly that health spending is by far the highest priority of Canadians. In more detail, the data on this type of spending show that a total of 83 percent advocates more spending on emergency health services—38 percent a lot more and 45 percent somewhat more. Similar responses were given on the issue of child health care. A total of 84 percent calls for more spending—37 percent a lot more and 47 percent somewhat more.

Education, the justice system, the environment, transportation, and CPP fall into a middling priority. Total support for these items is virtually as large as that for health care but the support is far less intense: far fewer Canadians advocate "a lot" more spending. Support for single mothers and university research trails slightly behind.

Figure 15: Where should government spend?—percent saying "a lot more" rather than "somewhat less" or "a lot less" in each area

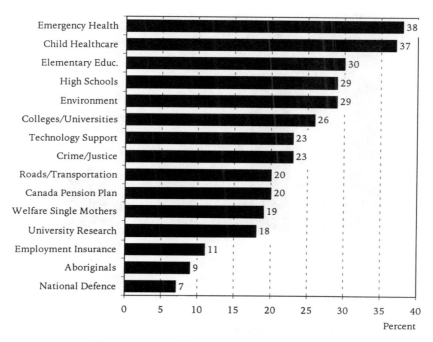

Source: COMPAS for Southam News, Winter, 1997/8.

Expenditures on aboriginal programs and defence have very low support. Thus, 35 percent advocate a greater priority for aboriginal programs (9 percent a lot, 26 percent somewhat more) while 30 percent call for somewhat less and 20 percent much less. The remainder call for no change. Seven percent of all Canadians want the government to spend a lot more on national defence, 23 percent somewhat more, 18 percent no change, 33 percent somewhat less, and 19 percent much less. These results are presented in figure 16, where the focus is on the proportion of those wanting lower and higher spending on the major programs.

Regional differences

Canada's provinces and regions agree on many large budgetary issues, for example how much of the surplus should go to debt repayment. But Canada's regions differ on spending priorities. Quebec and

Figure 16: Canadians, except aboriginals and members of Department of National Defence, want spending in education and health— percent saying "more money" versus those saying "less money"

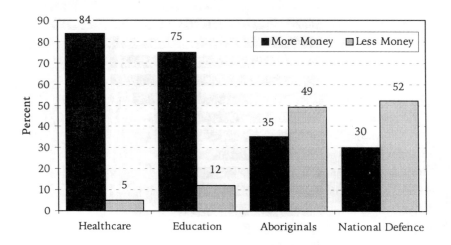

Source: COMPAS for Southam News, Winter, 1997/8.

Atlantic Canada favour a greater priority for social programs, including secondary education, emergency health services, and employment insurance.

The relative importance attached to social spending by different regions is clearly shown in figures 17, 18 and 19. Figure 17 shows what percent of the respondents want to spend a lot more on health care figure 18 shows regions that favour spending on high-school education. Ontarians are below the national mean but still quite far above Alberta and British Columbia. Figure 19 focuses on the differences between the Atlantic Provinces, Quebec, Ontario and the national average. The regional differences already noted show up even more strongly with respect to spending on employment insurance and help for single mothers.

British Columbians and Albertans are generally as opposed to increased spending as Ontarians with one notable exception. As figure 20 shows, 30 percent of respondents from British Columbia but only 23 percent of all Canadians want a lot more money spent on crime prevention and the justice system.

Figure 17: Easterners want more money spent on health—percent saying "a lot more money"

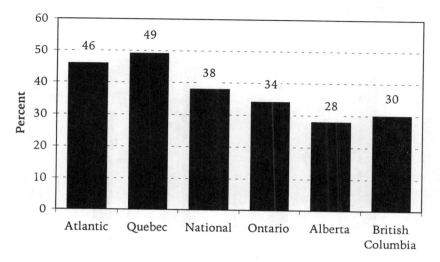

Source: COMPAS for Southam News, Winter, 1997/8.

Figure 18: Easterners want more money spent on high-school education—percent saying "a lot more money"

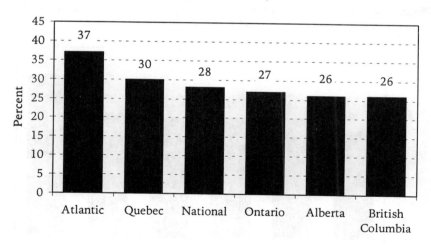

Source: COMPAS for Southam News, Winter, 1997/8.

Figure 19: Quebec and Atlantic provinces want increases in spending on social programs; Ontario does not—percent wanting "a lot more spending" in each area

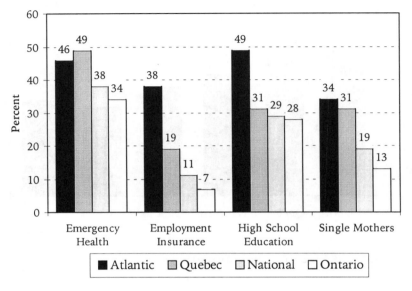

Source: COMPAS for Southam News, Winter, 1997/8.

Figure 20: Westerners want more money spent on crime prevention and justice system—percent saying "a lot more money"

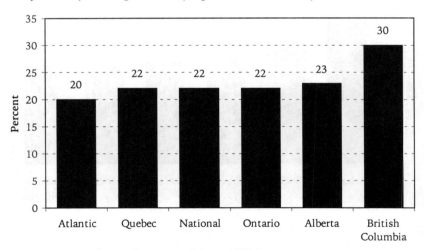

Source: COMPAS for Southam News, Winter, 1997/8.

Figure 21: Government should spend money on ... —percent agreeing "a lot" rather than "somewhat," "not really," or "not at all" for spending in each area

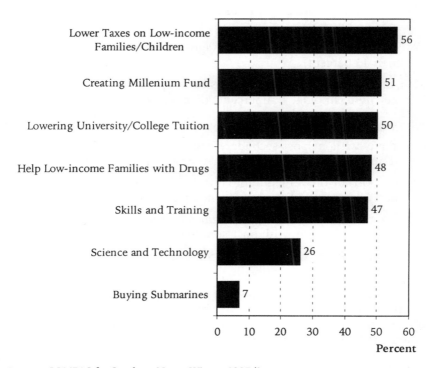

Source: COMPAS for Southam News, Winter, 1997/8.

Spending increases and current government initiatives

How popular are the spending and tax initiatives favoured by the current government? Figure 21 indicates that Canadians have a strong concern over the taxes paid by low-income families with children. This had already become apparent in the questions about the nature of tax reductions presented above. Help for families with low incomes and great costs for medical drugs ranks similarly high.

Figure 21 also shows strong support for programs to support higher education. Fifty-one percent agreed a lot with the creation of the so-called Millennium Fund, which would provide cheap loans for university and college students. Fifty percent agreed with policies for lower tuition for these students. Canadians also show strong support for more spending on skills and training. Support for science and technology was favoured much less and the purchase of submarines received very little support.

Gender

Women, on the one hand, showed a greater support than men for social expenditures. For example:

(1) creation of a Millennium Fund (agree a lot—women 56 percent, men 46 percent)

(2) lower post-secondary tuition (agree a lot—women 54 percent, men 45 percent).

Men, on the other hand, showed greater support for more spending on science and technology (34 percent) than women (19 percent).

Education and cultural differences

Canadians without post-secondary education are slightly more favorable to investments that provide more visible returns:

(1) support for the Millennium Fund (without post-secondary education 58 percent, with post-secondary education 46 percent).

(2) lower taxes for low-income families (without post-secondary education 62 percent, with post-secondary education 51 percent).

(3) Lower tuition (without post-secondary education 55 percent, with post-secondary education 46 percent).

The most educated are the least supportive of submarines: 20 percent of university graduates agree somewhat or a lot with a submarine purchase compared to 27 percent of those with some college or university education and 32 percent of those with high school or less.

Regional differences

There is a substantial national consensus on most of these issues. Among Quebecois, however, 75 percent agreed a lot that taxes should be lowered for low-income families with children while only 56 percent agreed a lot across the nation. Quebecois are also particularly supportive of allocations to help low-income families with drug purchases: 67 percent of Quebecois but only 48 percent across the nation agreed a lot with this statement. By the same relative amounts, Quebecois more than the entire population of Canada opposed spending money on submarines and approved the establishment of the Millennium Fund.

Age

Young and old differ moderately in their view of the current budget options in ways that reflect different economic interests and life-cycle perspectives. Fifty-eight percent of people under 30 years of age agree a lot that post-secondary tuition should be lowered compared to 50 percent of all Canadians and 46 percent of Canadians 60 years of age and older. Only 39 percent of Canadians under 30 years of age agree a lot that some of the surplus should go to skills and training compared to 47 percent of Canadians as a whole and 51 percent of those 50 years of age and older.

Younger adults, most of whom have yet to form families, are less supportive of lowering taxes for low-income families with children. Among the under-30 cohort, 47 percent agree a lot that taxes should be lightened on low-income families with children compared to 56 percent holding this view among Canadians as a whole and 63 percent among those over 50 years of age.

Conclusion

The single most important finding is that Canadians want paying down the debt to be the priority use for the federal surplus; tax reductions and program enhancements are secondary priorities. There is a nationwide consensus on this issue as there is on many other tax and spending issues. For example, Canadians are largely of one mind that high marginal tax rates are a disincentive to work.

The broad consensus among Canadians emerges from a shared ethical culture. There exists amazing agreement among Canadians in all regional and demographic groups on so many of the policy, tax, and expenditure challenges facing the federal government.

Economic self-interest rarely emerges as a transparent factor driving public attitudes. For example, high-income earners are not uniquely driven to favour lower taxes.

Modest subgroup differences do nonetheless come to the surface. These tend to reflect differences in cultural perspective like the post-1960s split that puts women to the left of the political spectrum and men to the right or the greater tendency of Quebecois to favour programs but abhor taxes.

Among all the issues probed in the massive Southan News effort, perhaps the most difficult was gauging Canadians' true attitudes towards taxes. On the one hand, Canadians seem much less inclined to favour tax reductions over debt repayment when asked what to do with the surplus. They are also less inclined to favour tax reductions than program enhancements. Yet, respondents seem irate, even angry, in their responses to questions that touch on the tax issue alone. Either Canadians are genuinely of two minds on tax and expenditure issues, or a certain political correctness has cowed them into under-reporting the depth of their aversion to taxes.

The Optimal Size
of Government and
Public Well-Being

Optimal Levels of Spending and Taxation in Canada

Johnny C.P. Chao and Herbert Grubel

Editor's Note: At the conference, How to Spend the Fiscal Dividend: What is the Optimal Size of Government? *(Ottawa, December 3, 1997), Professor Gerald Scully discussed his work, based on data from the United States and New Zealand, on the optimal level of government spending and taxation. His theoretical analysis as well as his empirical findings for these two countries provided an important and useful background for the day's discussion about the use of Canada's future fiscal surpluses but he does not have a written paper or empirical results based on Canadian data.*

The following chapter was prepared in order to ensure that Canadians have access to Professor Scully's ideas. It uses Scully's theoretical model and econometric approach as the basis for estimates of an optimal rate of taxation and government spending in Canada. This chapter draws upon The Optimum Levels of Spending and Taxation in Canada *by Johnny C.P. Chao and upon* The Growth Tax in Canada *by Joel Emes, Research Economist, and Dexter Samida, Research Assistant, at The Fraser Institute. Mr. Emes and Mr. Samida also provided assistance with the data and exposition of the final version.*

In recent years, many academic studies have examined both theoretically and empirically the relationship between government spending and economic growth. One approach considers factors known to influence economic growth—labour, education, capital, technology, price stability, and natural resources—for a set of countries and through time. The existence of systematic relationships between a country's growth rates and these variables has been established statistically. Some studies have

---

Notes will be found on page 67.

added the size of government to the more traditional list of determinants of economic growth. These studies have commonly found that the size of government matters but it is difficult to generalize from their results and to draw conclusions for individual countries because the data has been drawn from a number of countries.[1]

A second approach to the study of the role of government in economic growth concentrates on the experience of individual countries. It does not consider the types of determinants of economic growth but assumes instead that, whatever the determinants of economic growth, the size of government has an additional role to play. One of the pioneers in this field has been Gerald Scully, who has published his analyses of data from the United States and New Zealand as well as cross-country surveys of data from about 100 countries.[2] Professor Scully's methodology allowed him to give relatively precise estimates of the optimal size of government, finding it to be about 19 to 23 percent for the United States and New Zealand.

In this chapter we shall use Professor Scully's method to estimate the optimal size of government in Canada. In Part 1, we present a simple model to explain the economic forces that come into play at different levels of government spending and taxation. In Part 2, we present some historic data about spending by Canadian governments between 1929 and 1996. This data set is then used in econometric estimates using Professor Scully's model. The chapter closes with a discussion of the policy implications of our findings.

The concept of optimally sized government

In figure 1, the vertical axis measures the rate of economic growth and the horizontal axis measures government spending as a percent of national output. We assume that spending is equal to taxation. The line with the shape of an inverted U— the Scully curve—shows a postulated functional relationship between economic growth and the level of government spending in a given country.

The shape of the Scully curve g_aD in figure 1 can be explained using a simple analogy. Consider a piece of land in an arid region. The yield of corn planted on this land is increased by the initial application of water and fertilizer in small doses. Increasing the amount of water and fertilizer raises yields further but at a decreasing rate until ultimately the yield is maximized. Further application of water and fertilizer decreases yields and there comes a point where additional applications reduce output below the level at which it was before any water and fertilizer was applied. This relationship between inputs and outputs is described by the Scully curve in figure 1, assuming that the quantity of water and fertilizer are measured on the horizontal axis and yield on the vertical axis.

Figure 1: The Scully Curve

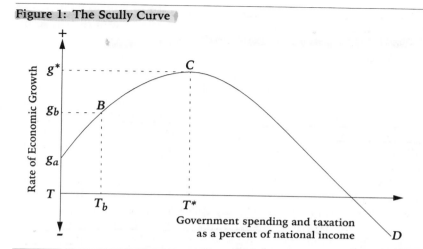

The economic analysis underlying the shape of the Scully curve is as follows. Consider first a zero level of government spending and taxation (T) associated with a growth rate g_a. This growth rate is low because the economy is inefficient when government supplies no services. Under these conditions, private agents have to provide for their own security, enforce contracts, set standards of measurement, and, generally, operate without the aid of the many public goods and services provided by modern states.

Now consider that, in this country with unchanged private sector supplies of capital, labour, and other resources, the government spends and taxes T_b percent of national income. It is postulated that this level of government activity brings about a growth rate of g_b. The higher growth is the result of the government's provision of public goods and services, which increase the overall economic efficiency of the private sector.

The higher efficiency is due to positive externalities (*i.e.* unpriced benefits) accruing to the private sector from the production of government services such as internal and external security, elementary schools, the judiciary, control of disease, roads, water supply, sewers, and a monetary authority assuring a monetary standard and monetary stability. At the low levels of taxation required for this level of spending, the disincentive effects of taxes on work, investment, and risk-taking are small.

Consider now a higher level of government spending and taxation, T^*, that yields a higher rate of economic growth, g^*. However, the curvature of the Scully line between B and C is such that the proportional increase in spending and taxation is less than the proportional increase in economic growth. This property of the curve suggests that government spending is subject to decreasing marginal returns.

Decreasing marginal returns characterize all economic activity. In the present case, they arise as government spending on individual projects at first meets the most pressing needs and exploits the most suitable opportunities for the replacement of inefficient private activities. As spending rises, additional projects financed by government become increasingly less productive. At some point, the marginal benefits from increased government spending become zero. This point is reached at T^* in figure 1, where spending by government produces the highest rate of economic growth the economy is capable of creating. Further increases in spending beyond T^* produce negative marginal effects on economic growth; the Scully curve turns down. In figure 1, we show economic growth falling to zero at a level of government spending, T_m. Higher spending beyond that point can produce negative rates of economic growth.

It is important to consider in more detail the forces that shape the Scully curve. First, there is the law of diminishing returns to additional government spending described in the preceding paragraph. Second, the withdrawal of resources from the private sector initially occurs at the cost of projects with low returns. But the more private spending is reduced, the higher the yield being sacrificed. So economic growth slows or turns down because of decreasing private sector output at growing marginal rates. Third, to raise revenue with which to finance government spending, governments have to impose taxes. Such taxation reduces the private sector's incentives to work, save, invest, and take risks. This, in turn, lowers economic growth.[3]

Finally, some of the spending programs can have additional and somewhat different disincentive effects if they lower the risk of economic life. For example, social security programs protecting workers from the adverse effects of unemployment, illness, and retirement cause them to change their behaviour and reduce work-effort, savings, and risk-taking. Such changes in economic behaviour decrease the effective supply of the traditional factors of production, labour, capital, and entrepreneurship, and therefore reduce economic growth.

Most economists would accept that the preceding analysis is valid and believe that the inverted-U shape of the Scully curve in figure 1 is a realistic description of the world. However, much less agreement exists about the precise curvature of the line and, especially, about the level of government spending at which the optimum growth rate g^* is attained.

Until recently, there were some who believed that the Scully curve rises over a wide range, levels off, and never turns down. These were supporters of communism, socialism and democratic socialism of the sort practised in Sweden and other countries of western Europe. Supporters of these economic systems believed that economic planning and command economies could operate efficiently and achieve rapid economic growth through large planned investment. They also believed that through education it would be possible to create "social man," who was immune to the disincentive effects of taxation and the availability of a wide range of government services. In fact, for a long time these people believed that countries with large governments could have higher rates of economic growth than those with mixed economies and small governments. After the fall of communism and the dismal economic record of social democracies like Sweden, the rank of such believers has shrunk greatly.

Gerald Scully estimated that, for the United States and New Zealand, the optimal level of government spending and taxation is in the range of 19 to 23 percent. Ludger Schuknecht and Vito Tanzi suggest in *Can Small Governments Secure Social and Economic Well-Being?* (this volume) that government spending in excess of 30 percent reduces economic growth and produces practically no additional improvement in social measures of well-being. What might the optimal rate be for Canada.

Evidence from Canadian data

In figure 2, we show for the years from 1929 to 1996 annual rates of real economic growth and government spending as a percent of national income for Canada. This graph shows that in the prewar period, rising from a low in 1933 during the Great Depression, Canada had both a high rate of economic growth and low levels of government spending. Growth remained high during and after World War II while spending remained around 25 percent of GDP. After about 1960, the size of government began to increase and continued to climb until 1996. During this period, the rate of economic growth was on a distinct downward trend. These data suggest at a simple and intuitive level that Canada around 1960 had reached its optimal level of spending and taxation—about 27 percent. Since in 1996 government spending was 48 percent of national income, Canadian governments clearly spent much more than the optimal amount.

The same impression is conveyed by figure 3, which presents in a different fashion the data underlying figure 2. Figure 3 measures the rate of economic growth on one axis and government spending as a percent of GDP on the other. The individual points represent annual observations of these two variables for the period from 1929 to 1996. It is not too difficult to visualize a Scully line in the shape of an inverted U running nicely through the thickest cluster of points in the graph.

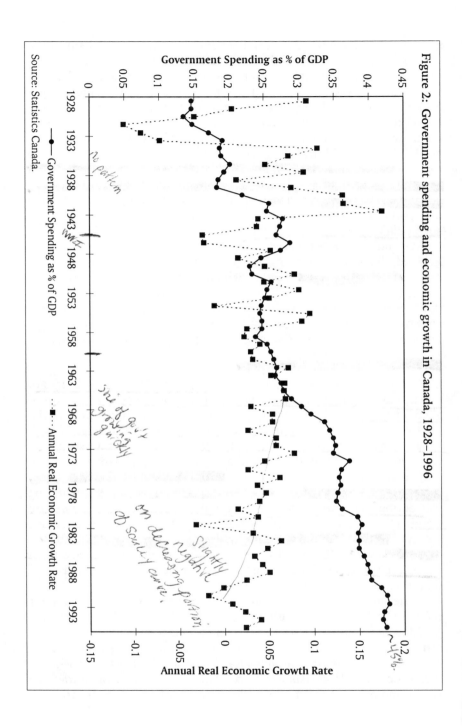

Figure 2: Government spending and economic growth in Canada, 1928–1996

Source: Statistics Canada.

Figure 3: Government spending and economic growth in Canada: scatter of annual observations

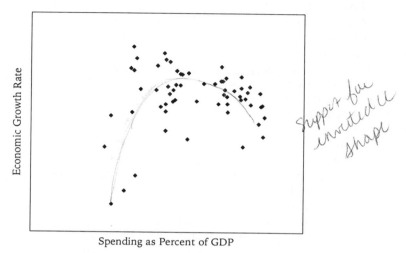

Source: Statistics Canada.

Fitting a quadratic equation

To estimate an optimal rate of government spending statistically Gerald Scully (1996) used a very simple and direct approach: he assumed that the data points fit a function described by the following equation:

$$x = a + bY = cY^2 \tag{1}$$

This equation has been found to describe many empirical phenomena in the world. It also is consistent with the law of diminishing returns since it approximates a line with the shape of an inverted U. Differentiating x in equation (1) with respect to Y and setting it zero shows the maximum point of the curve at $b/2c$.

Following Professor Scully, we substitute the economic growth rate g for x and the level of government spending and taxation τ for Y, we derive equation (2):

$$g = \alpha + \beta\tau + \gamma\tau^2 \tag{2}$$

Using a nonlinear regression, the results of which are given in the Appendix, we find that for Canada the optimal rate of spending and taxation is approximately 34 percent of national income.

A different model

Following Professor Scully again (1989, 1996) we can give a more sophisticated specification of the econometric model by assuming that economic growth is dependent upon the relative shares of national income spent by the government and the private sector. The mathematical formulation of the relationship uses a specific functional form known as the Cobb-Douglas production function. This production function is used widely in economics both because it describes accurately many empirical phenomena and because it has some convenient mathematical properties.

The economic growth rate is equal to output at time t divided by output in the preceding period: Y_t/Y_{t-1}, which can also be written as $1 + g$, where g is the percentage rate of economic growth. The growth rate is assumed to be determined by government spending in the preceding period G_{t-1} and by the amount spent by the private sector. The latter is determined by the rate of taxation τ and equal to $1 - \tau$ multiplied by that period's total national output Y_{t-1}. The Greek letters in equation (3) represent the relative magnitude that each of the elements contributes to economic growth; their magnitude is estimated econometrically from the data for Canada.[4]

$$\frac{Y_t}{Y_{t-1}} = 1 + g = \alpha \, (G_{t-1})^\beta \, (1 - \tau)^c \, (Y_{t-1})^{c-1} \tag{3}$$

In the Appendix, we present equation (3) differentiated once and twice with respect to the tax rate. The interpretation of these equations is that the basic function assumed to determine the growth rate has the properties postulated above, *i.e.*, government spending increases growth but at a decreasing rate until it reaches a maximum beyond which the growth rate is lowered.

We now simplify equation (3) by assuming that government spending G equals the amount of national income collected through taxes τY and derive the following equation:

$$1 + g = \alpha \tau^\beta (1 - \tau)^c \, (Y_{t-1})^{\beta + c - 1} \tag{4}$$

Differentiating g with respect to τ and setting it equal to zero we find equation (5), where τ^* is the growth maximizing rate of taxation.

$$\tau^* = \frac{\beta}{(\beta + c)} \tag{5}$$

Following normal procedures, we impose the restriction that the parameters represented by Greek letters in equation (4) sum to 1: $\beta + c = \beta + (1 - \beta) = 1$. This results in the simplified equation (6):

$$1 + g = \alpha \tau^{\beta} (1 - \tau)^{(1-\beta)} \tag{6}$$

Econometric estimates of this equation showed a high degree of collinearity between the dependent and independent variables. To deal with this problem, Gerald Scully (1996) divided both sides of the equation by $1 - \tau$ and obtained equation (7):

$$\frac{(1 + g)}{(1 - \tau)} = a \left[\frac{\tau}{(1 - \tau)} \right]^{\beta} \tag{7}$$

the log form of which gives equation (8):

$$\ln \left[\frac{(1 + g)}{(1 - \tau)} \right] = \ln\alpha + \ln \left[\frac{\tau}{(1 - \tau)} \right]^{\beta} \tag{8}$$

We used this equation and the annual data for Canada from 1926 to 1996. The results are presented in the Appendix for the simple ordinary least square regression. Several, more sophisticated, estimation techniques were used to correct for certain statistical problems associated with these original results.[5] These experiments improved the statistical reliability of the econometric results but did not affect the key result that the optimal rate of taxation and government spending in Canada is about 34 percent.

Conclusions and policy implications

The preceding analysis has some important implications for Canadian economic policy. In 1996, total spending by the governments of Canada was 48 percent of national income. The optimum rate of spending was estimated to be 34 percent. If spending were lowered by 29 percent to that optimum level, the rate of economic growth would increase. Our empirical study allows us to calculate by how big this increase would be.

The econometric results reported in Appendix 1a show that every one percent change in the ratio of spending to national income results in a .74 percent increase in the rate of economic growth.[6] The reduction in the spending ratio of 29 percent due to the movement to the optimal level results, therefore, in an increase in economic growth of 22 percent.

Figure 4: Economic growth at 3.0 percent and 3.7 percent

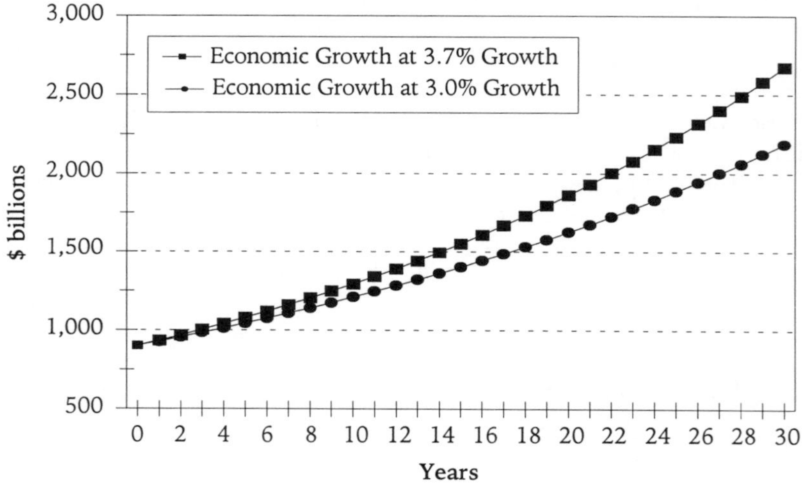

Source: Calculations by authors.

During the period 1990 to 1997, Canada's economy grew 3 percent annually. An increase of 22 percent of this rate brings it to 3.7 percent. The effects of such an increase in the rate of economic growth on national income can be seen in figure 4. At $900 billion in year zero (say 2000), 30 years later (in 2030) national income will be $2,677 billion if it grows at 3.7 percent and only $2,185 billion if it grows at 3.0 percent.

Figure 5 shows what happens to the absolute level of government spending under the two scenarios. The lower line shows that at time zero government spending is always equal to 34 percent of national income. Initially, government spending is at $306 billion, equal to 34 percent of national income of $900 billion. It grows 3.7 percent per year. The top line shows government spending at $432 billion or 48 percent of national income, growing at 3 percent annually. The graph shows that 51 years later the absolute levels of government spending would be the same under the two scenarios. Not shown is the important fact that thereafter government spending at 34 percent of national income would always be higher than under the assumption that it is 48 percent of national income.

Figure 6 shows what happens to private income under the two scenarios. The bottom line represents an initial private income of $468 billion, equal to 52 percent of total national income. It grows at 3 percent and reaches a level of $2,177 billion in 51 years. The top line shows that,

Figure 5: Government spending at 3.0 percent and 3.7 percent growth

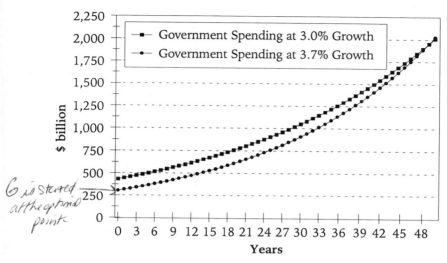

Source: Calculations by authors.

if private spending were raised to $586 billion, equal to 66 percent of total national income, the accompanying growth rate of 3.7 percent in 51 years would yield an income of $2,763 billion, or $586 billion more than under the first scenario. It is important to remember that, in this fifty-first year under the optimum government spending strategy, the absolute level of government spending would also be the same as it would have been had it stayed at its present sub-optimal level.

The preceding figures are only illustrative and assume that all other influences on economic growth remain the same. But they do indicate that reductions in the size of government relative to total national income would significantly raise the private income of future generations and eventually permit greater government spending without impingement on private spending.

The facts brought out by the preceding analysis should be given serious consideration when decisions are made about the use of the fiscal surpluses expected in the future. To reduce government spending from 48 to 34 percent of national income, spending increases have to be below the growth in national income. The remaining surpluses must go to the reduction of taxes and debt. The greater the share of the surpluses going to these expenditure reductions, the more rapidly the country will reach its optimum level of spending and enjoy a corresponding increase in the rate of economic growth.

Figure 6: Private income at 3.0 percent and 3.7 percent growth

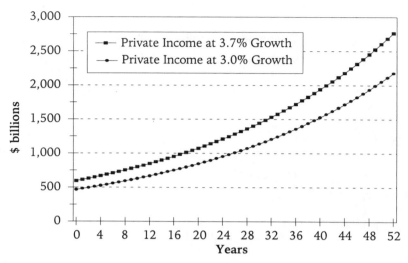

Source: Calculations by authors.

Appendix 1A

Summary estimates for

$$\ln\left[\frac{(1+g)}{(1-\tau)}\right] = \ln\alpha + \ln\left[\frac{\tau}{(1-\tau)}\right]^{\beta}$$

Ordinary least squared regression summary statistics

R	.919
R Square	.844
Adjusted R Square	.841
Standard Error of the Estimate	.07032
Mean LN_DPVR1	.4844
Mean LN_IPVR1	−.7470
Standard Deviation LN_DPVR1	.1766
Standard Deviation LN_IPVR1	.4804

Appendix 1B

Summary estimates for

$$1 + g = \alpha + \beta_1\tau + \beta_2\tau^2$$

Constrained non-linear regression summary statistics

Source	DF	Sum of Squares	Mean Square
Regression	3	80.10837	26.70279
Residual	66	.33283	5.042917E-03
Uncorrected Total	69	80.44120	
(Corrected Total)	68	.35580	

R squared = 1 – Residual SS/Corrected SS = .06454
Asymptotic 95%

Asymptotic Confidence Interval

Parameter	Estimate	Standard Error	Lower	Upper
A	.864523201	.100132568	.664602078	1.064444323
B	1.326296262	.625955843	.076535099	2.576057425
C	-1.885825758	.912990020	-3.708669147	-.062982369

Appendix 1C

Summary estimates for

$$1 + g = \alpha\tau^{\beta}(1 - \tau)^{(1-\beta)} \tag{9}$$

Nonlinear Regression Summary Statistics

Source	DF	Sum of Squares	Mean Square
Regression	2	80.09560	40.04780
Residual	67	.34561	5.158311E-03
Uncorrected Total	69	80.44120	
(Corrected Total)	68	.35580	

R squared = 1 – Residual SS/Corrected SS = .02864
Asymptotic 95%

Asymptotic Confidence Interval

Parameter	Estimate	Standard Error	Lower	Upper
A	2.092074523	.031599164	2.029002327	2.155146720
B	.337247995	.017251433	.302813992	.371681999

Appendix 2A

First and second degree derivatives of

$$\frac{Y_t}{Y_{t-1}} = 1 + g = \alpha \, (G_{t-1})^\beta \, (1 - \tau)^c \, (Y_{t-1})^{c-1}$$

Taking the derivatives of g with respect to G, the marginal productivities of increasing government expenditures at a positive but diminishing rate may be revealed. Conversely, for τ denotes the average tax rate, increasing taxation levels negatively affects the rate growth at an increasing rate. Hence, with respect to G,

$$\frac{\partial g}{\partial G} = \alpha G^{\beta-1} \, Y^{c-1} \, \beta (1 - \tau)^c$$

$$\frac{\partial^2 g}{\partial G^2} = \alpha \beta G^{\beta-2} \, Y^{c-1} \, (1 - \tau)^c \, (\beta - 1)$$

where $\partial g / \partial G > 0$ and $\partial^2 g / \partial G^2 < 0$. Further, with respect to τ,

$$\frac{\partial g}{\partial \tau} = \alpha G^\beta \, Y^{c-1} \, (1 - \tau)^{c-1} c$$

$$\frac{\partial^2 g}{\partial \tau^2} = \alpha c G^\beta \, Y^{c-1} \, (1 - \tau)^{c-2} \, (c - 1)$$

where $\partial g / \partial \tau > 0$ and $\partial^2 g / \partial \tau^2 < 0$. These transformations charts out the curvature approximation akin to those depicted in figure 3, and forms the empirical basis behind both the Laffer and Scully Curves.

Notes

1 One of the most respected efforts using this approach is by Barro (1990, 1991, 1996). Others are Grier and Tullock (1980); Tanzi and Schuknecht (1995).

2 See Scully 1989, 1995, 1996.

3 The similarity between the preceding Scully curve and the well-known Laffer curve is no coincidence. The Laffer curve (named after the American economist who developed it in the late 1960s) shows the relationship between total government revenue and rates of taxation. It is also drawn as an inverted U for the following reasons. At zero tax rates, revenues are zero; at 100 percent tax rates, revenues are also zero because incentives to work are totally destroyed if the government confiscates all of the income earned. As tax rates rise from zero, revenues increase initially. However, as a matter of logical necessity, since at a rate of 100 percent they are zero, at some level of rates they must reach a maximum and then decline.

4 As will be discussed below, the basic assumptions used to justify the existence and shape of both the Laffer and the Scully curves are accepted by most analysts. The central question about the Laffer curve is empirical and often heatedly debated. At what level of taxation is revenue maximized in Canada? Are current rates above or below that point of maximization? The same issue surrounds the Scully curve. What is the optimal size of government?

5 Additional statistical inferences were made based on the testing model as proposed by equation (8). These tests included both constrained and unconstrained nonlinear regressions on equations (1) and (6), with insignificant differences in the imputed results. As it is common in economics that there may be several competing theories that attempt to explain the same set of variables, a non-nested hypothesis was conducted to evaluate the statistical validities of equations (1)and (8). Non-nested hypotheses work through the exploitation of the falsity of other models, such that one specification cannot contribute any more explanatory power on the independent variable than the 'true' model. Again, the variance in the value of the optimal level of government spending and taxation as derived was found to be insignificant, and our approaches here remain statistically valid.

6 The slope of the independent variable in log form in equation (8) can be interpreted directly as the elasticity.

References

Barro, R.J. (1990). Government Spending in a Simple Model of Endogenous Growth. *Journal of Political Economy* 98: 103–25.

——— (1991). Economic Growth in a Cross Section of Countries. *Quarterly Journal of Economics* (May): 407–43.

Chao, Johnny C.P. (1997). The Optimum Levels of Spending and Taxation in Canada. Unpublished paper. Department of Economics, Simon Fraser University.

Emes, Joel, and Dexter Samida (1997). The Growth Tax in Canada. Unpublished paper. The Fraser Institute.

Grier, Kevin, and Gordon Tullock (1980). An Empirical Analysis of Cross-national Economic Growth, 1951–80. *Journal of Monetary Economics* 24: 259–76.

Scully, Gerald (1989). The Size of the State, Economic Growth and the Efficient Utilization of National Resources. *Public Choice* 63: 149–64.

——— (1995). The "Growth Tax" in the United States. *Public Choice* 85: 71–80.

——— (1996). Taxation and Economic Growth in New Zealand. *Pacific Economic Review* 1, 2 (September): 169–77.

Tanzi, Vito, and Ludger Schuknecht (1995). The Growth of Government and the Reform of the State in Industrial Countries. *IMF Working Paper* (December).

Can Small Governments Secure Economic and Social Well-Being?

VITO TANZI AND LUDGER SCHUKNECHT

The appropriate role and size of government has been debated amongst economists since the period of classical economics and *laissez-faire* in the nineteenth century. However, economic thinking and policies have changed considerably over the past century. Public spending began to increase as two world wars expanded the revenue bases, as social security systems began to develop, and as public spending programs were introduced during and after the Great Depression. The period after World War II witnessed much faith in the ability of governments to improve people's economic and social well-being through higher spending. The result was an unprecedented growth—especially in the 1960s and 1970s—in public expenditure in most industrialized countries.

In more recent years, however, scepticism has grown about what governments can, in fact, do to alleviate social and economic problems. Publications by those studying public choice and political economy

The views expressed in this paper are those of the authors and should not be interpreted as representing official positions of the International Monetary Fund or of the World Trade Organisation. We would like to thank Solita Wakefield and Anne Hughes for their assistance. Notes will be found on pages 89–90.

provided theoretical and empirical reasons for this scepticism; Margaret Thatcher and Ronald Reagan exploited this scepticism to promote their political objectives. While the more ideological debate of the early 1980s has given way to a more reasoned assessment of the size and efficiency of government activity, "lean" governments and "balanced" (or near balanced) budgets have once again become popular.[1]

What have been the driving forces for this re-assessment of the role of government? Economic thinking changed as theoretical models and empirical evidence put into doubt the possible benefits to be achieved from an activist state. The experiences of some newly industrialized countries with very small public sectors and rapid growth contrasted visibly with growing public spending and debt, rising real interest rates, and slow growth in many industrialized countries. Aging populations and their impact upon spending on public health and pensions began to add a sense of urgency to the mounting fiscal problems. Globalization and growing competition for international capital have made countries with large public sectors and high taxes less attractive to international investors. All these factors have increased the pressure upon governments to become smaller and more efficient, and to balance their books.

In the past two years, however, a new strand of thinking has emerged, claiming that globalization, fiscal reform, and liberalization will reduce the governments' ability to provide basic services and social safety nets. It is argued that economic and social well-being will suffer as governments are forced to down-size, with potentially serious consequences for the poor and for social stability. As a consequence, these authors recommend a large array of often poorly justified interventions that include more public spending and protectionism.[2]

We shall argue that countries with "small" governments generally do not show worse indicators of social and economic well-being than countries with "big" governments—and often they achieve an even better standard. Countries with "small" governments can provide essential services and minimum social safety nets while avoiding the disincentive effects caused by high taxes and large-scale redistribution on growth, employment, and welfare. If there is a normative conclusion arising from our analysis, it is that fiscal reform and lower public spending should be possible in many countries without sacrificing much social and economic well-being. The resistance to these reforms, however, is more the result of vested interests than of their effect upon welfare.

The chapter is structured as follows: section 1 briefly outlines the historical development of public spending in industrial countries; section 2 compares social and economic indicators as affected by public spending in industrial and newly industrialized countries; section 3 looks at distributional indicators across countries and section 4 analyzes the economic performance of different groups of countries; section 5 compares a selection of countries with small governments in more detail; and section 6 concludes with a brief examination of reforms in a number of industrialized and newly industrialized countries.

History of the growth of government

The public sectors of today's industrialized countries once absorbed a much smaller share of resources than they do at present. Table 1 illustrates that government spending during the late nineteenth and early twentieth century averaged less than 12 percent of GDP, or only about a quarter of today's level. A century ago, Japan, The Netherlands, Norway, and the United States reported levels of public expenditure less than 10 percent of GDP. France was even considered as having a "very big" government at 12.6 percent of GDP (Leroy-Beaulieu 1888). A large share of the budget was spent on the military, essential public works, and on government administration. In this period, universal public primary education, major investment projects, and embryonic social safety security systems were introduced in many countries; economies were thriving and poverty was declining (Connell 1980; Altenstetter 1986).

World War I and the Great Depression started the departure from this pattern of low public spending and laissez-faire policies. To finance their participation in the first World War, several countries extended their revenue base considerably. After the war, the larger tax base allowed governments to maintain higher expenditure levels, in part to pay for war-related debt and reparations (Peacock and Wiseman 1960). As a consequence, public expenditure increased in 1920 to an average of nearly 20 percent of GDP, with governments in France, Germany, New Zealand, or the United Kingdom spending about one-quarter of GDP. The Great Depression of the early 1930s resulted in a new, significant wave of programs of public expenditure, including the New Deal in the United States. The Great Depression was considered as a major failure of laissez-faire. Furthermore, a number of countries were soon engaged in wars or preparations for war, so that by 1937 public spending had edged up to an average of 23 percent, reaching 30 percent in France, Germany, and the United Kingdom. However, Norway, Spain, and Sweden still reported levels of public expenditure well below 20 percent of GDP.

The period since World War II and, in particular, between 1960 and 1980 saw a rapid increase in public spending. This increase is particularly remarkable because it took place during a period when most countries were not engaged in war efforts. John Maynard Keynes's

Table 1: Growth of general government expenditure in industrialized

Country	1870	1913	1920
General government for all years			
Australia	18.3	16.5	19.3
Austria	...	...	14.7[b]
Canada	...	...	16.7
France	12.6	17.0	27.6
Germany	10.0	14.8	25.0
Ireland	...	...	18.8
Japan	8.8	8.3	14.8
New Zealand	...	...	24.6
Norway	5.9	9.3	16.0
Sweden	5.7	10.4	10.9
Switzerland	16.5	14.0	17.0
United Kingdom	9.4	12.7	26.2
United States	7.3	7.5	12.1
Average	10.5	12.3	18.7
Central government for 1870 – 1937, general government thereafter			
Belgium	...	13.8	22.1
Italy	11.9	11.1	22.5
Netherlands	9.1	9.0	13.5
Spain	...	11.0	8.3
Average	10.5	11.2	16.6
Total Average	10.5	11.9	18.2

Sources: Vito Tanzi and Ludger Schuknecht (1997a), Reconsidering the Fiscal Role of Government: The International Perspective, American Economic Review, 87:164-168; and OECD (1997) Economic Outlook, Paris.

a In some cases, pre-World War II data have been calculated on the basis of GNP or NNP instead of GDP.

b Central-government data for this year.

c Data refer to 1970.

countries, 1870–1996 (percentage of GDP)[a]

1937	1960	1980	1990	1996
14.8	21.2	34.1	34.7	36.6
20.6	35.7	48.1	48.6	51.7
25.0	28.6	38.8	46.0	44.7
29.0	34.6	46.1	49.8	54.5
34.1	32.4	47.9	45.1	49.0
25.5	28.0	48.9	41.2	42.0
25.4	17.5	32.0	31.7	36.2
25.3	26.9[b,c]	38.1	41.3	34.7
11.8	29.9	43.8	54.9	49.2
16.5	31.0	60.1	59.1	64.7
24.1	17.2	32.8	33.5	39.4
30.0	32.2	43.0	39.9	41.9
19.7	27.0	31.4	32.8	33.3
23.2	27.9	41.9	43.0	44.5
21.8	30.3	57.8	54.8	54.3
24.5	30.1	42.1	53.2	52.9
19.0	33.7	55.8	54.0	49.9
13.2	18.8	32.2	42.0	43.3
19.6	28.2	47.0	51.0	50.1
22.4	27.9	43.1	44.9	45.8

The General Theory of Employment, Interest, and Money (1936), Richard A. Musgrave's *The Theory of Public Finance: A Study in Public Economy* (1959), and John Kenneth Galbraith's influential book *The Affluent Society* (1958) suggested expansions in the allocative, redistributional, and stabilizing roles of government. These approaches were built on the assumption that expansionary expenditure programs could identify and target potential beneficiaries at low administrative cost and high efficiency (Tanzi 1986). Most studies at that time did not find any negative impact upon the economy by the very high marginal tax rates prevailing at the time.

In addition, institutional provisions for accommodating interventionist policies were introduced in national constitutions or through the legislature and national court systems (Moser 1994). The growth of government was also facilitated by the dynamics of the political process in democratic societies (Forte and Peacock 1985; Mueller 1986; Buchanan, Rowley, and Tollison 1987; Alesina and Perotti 1995a).

This historical and institutional perspective is essential in explaining the growth in public spending after World War II. Initially, public expenditure increased relatively slowly to an average of only 28 percent of GDP by 1960. The Scandinavian countries expanded public spending more rapidly during this period whereas Germany, Japan, or Switzerland had smaller governments than they had before World War II. The public spending of less than 20 percent of GDP recorded in Japan and Switzerland in 1960 was, in fact, comparable to the levels of public expenditure prevailing in the newly industrialized countries today.

Between 1960 and 1980, public spending increased very rapidly, growing from 28 percent of GDP in 1960 to 43 percent of GDP by 1980. In Belgium, the Netherlands, and Sweden, the government spent over 50 percent of GDP by 1980. In the following period, growth in expenditure slowed down but there was no decrease in most countries. Public spending averaged 45 percent of GDP in 1990 and 46 percent in 1996. In very recent years, a number of countries started fiscal reforms aimed at reducing public spending—notably New Zealand and, among the newly industrialized countries, Chile (Tanzi and Schuknecht 1997b). However, several other countries—including Canada, Ireland, the Netherlands—have also started reducing public spending.

Examining the changing composition of expenditure will also help us to understand better what has driven the growth of public sectors in industrialized countries. Between the late nineteenth century and 1960, about one-half of public expenditure was on public consumption. Since 1960, however, this share has declined to 40 percent. The other main spending category that witnessed a decline is public investment: it absorbed 20 percent of total spending a century ago, but accounted for hardly more than 5 percent of total spending in the 1990s.

The most important increase in spending has been recorded for transfers and subsidies (which are the main ingredients of the so-called welfare-state spending). Income transfers and subsidies amounted to about 10 percent of the much lower total spending in the late nineteenth century. This share increased to half of all spending today, as limited social-safety nets have often been transformed into universal entitlement programs. Spending on transfers and subsidies increased most rapidly in the past 35 years, from an average of less than 10 percent of GDP in 1960 to 23 percent of GDP in 1995. This is equivalent to about three-quarters of the total expenditure increase since 1960. In addition, frequent fiscal deficits and growing public debt have boosted governments' interest obligations in almost all industrialized countries. Interest spending reached 10 percent of GDP or 20 percent of total spending in Belgium and Italy in the early 1990s, or almost as much as their total spending in 1913.

Government revenue increased in tandem with public expenditure until the 1960s—until then, balanced budgets prevailed. In the 1970s and 1980s, however, many countries developed persistent fiscal deficits, as revenue increased less quickly then spending. Public sector revenue in the 1990s averages over 40 percent of GDP. This is a remarkable level of revenue collection that most economists would not have thought possible only 50 years ago.[3] However, it requires high marginal and average rates of taxation, and still does not cover spending in most industrial countries.

The size of government and the public production of goods and services

One way of answering the question whether small governments can secure economic and social well-being is by comparing social and economic indicators between countries and groups of countries. As public policies affect these indicators, the latter can illustrate different standards of government performance. For easier comparison between country groups, we divide the countries in table 1 into three groups.[4] In "big" government countries, public spending exceeded 50 percent of GDP in 1990. "Medium" governments reported public spending between 40 and 50 percent of GDP. "Small" governments showed government expenditure of less than 40 percent of GDP. A fourth group includes the "newly industrialized economies" of Chile, Korea, Singapore, and Hong Kong, which by these standards all report "very small" governments.

The upper part of table 2 illustrates the difference in levels of total spending and in the composition of expenditure between the country groups in about 1990. The lower part reports on socio-economic indicators that are presumably affected by public expenditure. Public spending

Table 2: The size of government and the production of goods and services (about 1990).

	Size of government			
	Big[1]	Medium[2]	Small[3]	Very Small[4]
Total Public Expenditure (% of GDP)	55.1	44.9	34.6	18.6
Consumption	18.9	17.4	15.5	9.1
Investment	2.4	2.0	2.2	2.7
Expenditure by Function				
Health	6.6	5.9	5.2	1.8
Education	6.4	5.6	5.0	3.3
Administrative Efficiency (10 = best, 0 = worst score)				
Judiciary system	9.3	8.6	10.0	8.3
Red tape	8.1	7.8	9.0	8.9
Corruption	8.2	8.2	8.1	7.2
Education				
Illiteracy rate	1.2	1.2	1.0	5.9
Secondary school enrolment (in%)	96	100	92	85
Average mathematical achievement[5]	515	523	533	607
Tertiary enrolment ratio for women 18–23 years (value = 100)	101	79	100	76
Health				
Life expectancy	77	77	77	75
Infant mortality 1,000 births	6.7	7.1	6.4	8.6

Sources: Mauro (1995); OECD (1996); Tanzi and Schuknecht (1998); Transparency International (1996); UN, Human Development Report (various issues); World Bank, World Development Indicators (1997).

1 Belgium; Italy; The Netherlands; Norway; Sweden (public expenditure more than 50 per cent of GDP in 1990).
2 Austria; Canada; France; Germany; Ireland; New Zealand; Spain (public expenditure between 40 and 50 per cent of GDP in 1990).
3 Australia; Japan; Switzerland; United Kingdom; United States (public expenditure less than 40 per cent of GDP in 1990).
4 Newly industrialized economies: Chile, Hong Kong, China, Korea, Singapore.
5 International median = 500; 8th grade students, 1994; Korea only from newly industrialized countries.

in countries with "big" government averaged 55 percent of GDP compared to about 35 percent of GDP for countries with "small" governments. The corresponding figure is less than 20 percent of GDP for the newly industrialized economies. But, the Asian crisis revealed that budgetary spending in these countries did not always cover all public sector obligations such as implicit financial liabilities. The difference in public expenditure on goods and services (government consumption), however, was much less significant. Government consumption of 18.9 percent in countries with large public sectors was 3.4 percentage points higher than in countries with small public sectors. Nevertheless, "thrifty" governments spend only about 10 to 15 percent of GDP on government consumption, compared to 20 or more percent of GDP by some of the big spenders. Health and education are two of the important components of government consumption in most countries.[5] Spending by newly industrialized countries on government consumption is similar to that of some industrialized countries with low public spending. However, they report the highest outlays on public investment, higher than that of all groups of industrialized countries.

Adam Smith identified public administration as one of the key roles of government and all groups receive relatively high scores. However, the country group with small governments features the most efficient judiciaries and the least red tape, with near perfect scores for all countries. Corruption is limited in most industrialized countries, and indices of corruption are similar across country groups. The newly industrialized countries show better scores than most industrialized countries for red tape but slightly poorer scores for judicial efficiency and corruption. The relatively high scores in these areas reflect a functioning public administration that provides adequate public services and secures property rights.

The public provision of many health and education services is also seen as one of the key roles of government. The governments of the industrialized countries typically spend between 5 and 7 percent of their GDP on public education and on public health. Spending of education and health care is 1.5 percent of GDP (or 20 percent) higher in countries with big governments than in those with small public sectors. However, public spending on education in industrialized countries is almost twice as high as it is in newly industrialized countries, and spending on health is almost three times as high. Furthermore, in industrialized countries public spending in these areas has doubled since 1960 when public spending for education was only 3.5 percent of GDP and spending for health was 2.4 percent of GDP. (These amounts are similar to those for today's newly industrialized countries.) Part of the increase in public spending in industrialized countries is probably due to the ageing of the population, which raises the costs of health care.

However, more generous public support for health care systems, more public provision of education, and free secondary and tertiary education in many countries have probably also contributed to the increase.

Performance indicators are quite similar across groups of countries for health and education. Literacy, secondary school enrollment, infant mortality, and life expectancy are relatively uniform across industrialized countries. Medium-sized governments trail behind somewhat in tertiary school enrollment for women. Educational attainment (as measured by the mathematical scores of eighth graders attending secondary school) is highest in countries with small governments.

Newly industrialized countries show lower indicators for literacy, and for secondary school enrollment. It is remarkable, however, that the educational standards in Korea are significantly higher than in all industrialized countries. In fact, the international comparison of education levels awards top ranks to Japan and Korea whereas other industrial countries trail behind (OECD 1996).

The size of government and the redistribution of income

We mentioned above that most of the growth in public expenditure in industrialized countries since 1960 was on account of transfers and subsidies. This spending category also shows the most pronounced difference between groups of countries. Countries with big governments apply over 30 percent of GDP to transfers and subsidies (table 3). This is more than twice the 14 percent recorded for countries with small public sectors. Almost every third dollar earned in the first group is redistributed through the public sector in the form of cash transfers to consumers. Transfers and subsidies in all industrial countries, without exception, are considerably higher than in the newly industrialized countries. In the latter group, only 6 percent of GDP is spent on this category. This spending pattern illustrates that voters in many industrialized countries have given a very strong redistributive role to their governments.

Historical data on income distribution can help us understand the effects of redistribution. The earliest data we could find are from the 1910s or 1920s and include only a handful of countries. Table 4 illustrates the ratio of income of the top 10 percent of the labour force compared to the median income of the labour force. The table indicates that in all countries incomes have become more compressed during this century. While in the 1920s and 1930s the top 10 percent earned two to three and one-half times more than the median, this ratio had declined to about two times the median by the 1960s and did not change much until the mid-1970s. Wage compression continued after 1960 only in Switzerland. Austria, Norway, and Sweden reported the most

Table 3: The size of government and distributional indicators in different country groups (about 1990)

	Size of government			
	Big [1]	Medium	Small	Newly Industrialized
Public expenditure (% GDP)				
Subsidies and transfers	30.6	21.5	14.0	5.7
Income distribution				
Income share of lowest 40% of households	20.1	18.7	17.3	15.3
Share of transfers to poorest 20% of households[2]	22.2	25.2	33.6	...
Income equalization via taxation and transfers poorest 40% of households[3]	2.7	2.2	2.1	...
Employment				
Unemployment rate[4]	8.5	11.9	6.6	2.9

Sources: IMF, GFS (1996); OECD (1995); World Bank, World Development Indicators (1997); Zandarakili (1994).
[1] Belgium; Italy; The Netherlands; Norway; Sweden (public expenditure more than 50 per cent of GDP in 1990).
[2] 1980s for most countries.
[3] About 1980, as percent of total income.

egalitarian wage structure in the 1970s but differences among the 7 countries were very small by that time. The figures show that much equalization in the income distribution took place before 1960. Wage equalization and the introduction of basic social legislation and social insurance led Galbraith to observe already in 1958 that "the basic uncertainties of life had been eliminated" (Galbraith 1958: ch. 8). This was when government spending on transfers and subsidies averaged less than 10 percent of GDP.

Looking at income distribution and public expenditure in the 1990s, we can find a number of interesting patterns. First, the income distribution has become somewhat more equal than it was in 1960 (World Bank 1997). It is also more equal in countries with big governments than in those with small public sectors. We use the income share of the poorest 40 percent of households as a measure of income

Table 4: Ratio of income of the top 10 percent of labour force to the median income

	1920s	1930s	1960	Mid-1970s
Austria	2.0	...	1.9	1.9
Denmark	2.8	2.7	2.0	2.0
Germany	2.4[1]	...	2.2	2.1
The Netherlands	...	2.5[2]	2.1	2.0
Norway	3.4	...	2.0	1.8
Sweden	2.5	3.0	1.9	1.9
Switzerland	...	...	2.8	2.0
Average	2.6	...	2.1	2.0

Source: Flora, Kraus and Pfering (1987).
[1] 1913
[2] 1946

distribution.[6] Table 3 shows that this group of households in countries with big governments have 20 percent of national income at their disposal. This share is, on average, 2.8 percentage points higher than in countries with small governments but in some cases there is no difference at all. Therefore, the question should be asked whether this marginal difference in the distribution of income justifies public spending levels which are on average 20 percent of GDP higher (55 percent as compared to 35 percent). Newly industrialized countries report a more unequal income distribution on average. However, Chile's indicator depresses considerably the average for this group whereas Korea shows more equal income distribution than most industrialized countries.

The results reported above suggest that public expenditure may often be a relatively inefficient instrument for equalizing incomes. The reasons for this can be seen in rows 2 and 3 of Table 3. Transfers are much better targeted in countries with small public sectors. In countries with big public sectors, only 22 percent of transfers benefit the poorest quintile. In France or Sweden, more than 20 percent of transfers go to the richest 20 percent of households (OECD, 1995).[7] In countries with small governments, one-third of transfers reaches the poorest quintile, and Australia and Switzerland report as much as 40 percent. Zandavakili (1994) has estimated that income equalization for the poorest 40 percent of households as a result of transfers and taxation has been less than 3 percent in countries with large public sectors, hardly one percent more than in countries with small public sectors.

The poor targeting of transfers in countries with big governments seems to have created a "machinery" for reshuffling money between social groups with winners and losers not being clearly identifiable. This and the efficiency losses associated with redistribution has led Palda (1997) to conclude that equal cuts in public spending and in taxes would be beneficial to a large share of the population in industrialized countries. He calls the current situation "fiscal churning" and estimates that this unnecessary spending amounts to several percent of GDP in Canada.

Income distribution, however, is not only determined by government tax and transfer policies. The even distribution of human capital across societies is seen as another, perhaps even more important, equalizer of income that can be achieved without much government intervention beyond public support for education. Furthermore, human capital helps people climb up the income ladder. Table 5 reports some simple ordinary-least-squares (OLS) regression results for the effect of government redistribution and human capital on income distribution. The coefficient of the "transfers and subsidies" variable (as a proxy for

Table 5: Regression Analysis of Income Distribution

Dependent Variable: Income Distribution[1]

Independent Variables coefficient (t-statistic)	Estimate 1	Estimate 2	Estimate 3
Constant	1.84 (0.43)	1.63 (0.38)	−5.33 (0.77)
Public transfers and subsidies	0.11 (1.98)		0.16 (3.12)**
Total public spending		0.07 (1.75)	
Secondary school enrolment	0.15 (3.12)**	0.15 (2.98)*	
Educational attainment[2]			0.04 (3.16)**
Number of observations	18	18	15
R^2 adjustment	0.52	0.49	0.48

[1] Income share of poorest 40 percent of households.
[2] Variable comprises average national scores in mathematical achievement test, 8th grade students.
* = significant at the 95 percent level; ** = significant at the 99 percent level.

redistribution) is significant (in estimation 1 only marginally so) but the coefficient of the "total public spending" variable is insignificant in explaining differences in income distribution across industrialized countries. Both variables for human capital, *i.e.* secondary school enrollment and educational attainment are significant for explaining income distribution. The coefficient of the secondary school enrollment variable suggests that a 10 percent higher enrollment rate increases the income share of the poorest 40 percent of households by 1.5 percent. An average educational standard that is 10 points (or 2 percent) better improves income distribution by 0.4 percent. These results are intuitive because a higher secondary school enrollment rate or average educational attainment is likely to benefit the poorer segments of society most.[8]

Another issue is the distribution of employment within societies. It has been claimed that in many countries, wages of low-skilled labour are kept artificially high, thereby raising unemployment rates. Generous social-security benefits reduce the incentives for the unemployed to look for work (for a survey, see Lindbeck 1996).[9] Unemployment, especially unemployment among youths and long-term unemployment, also undermines equality of opportunity, as the unemployed have little opportunity to better their situation. There is some evidence that unemployment is more prevalent in countries with big and medium-sized governments. Unemployment in countries with small public sectors averaged 6.6 percent in 1996, compared to 8.5 and 11.9 percent in the other two groups of countries. It is also not surprising that unemployment in the newly industrialized countries is very low—less than 3 percent.

The adverse personal and social consequences of unemployment—especially unemployment among youths and long-term unemployment—should probably be added to the social costs of high government spending when the trade-off between higher public spending with more equal income distribution on the one hand is compared with smaller public spending with less equal income distribution on the other hand. More importantly, the same benefits for the poor can be reached with fewer public transfers or subsidies, if public spending is better targeted. We will see below that Japan, Korea, and Switzerland report a relatively more equal income distribution while their total public spending and transfers are much lower than in other industrialized countries with less even income distribution.

The size of government and economic performance

The last group of indicators compares the economic performance of the groups of countries. Table 6 shows that over the period from 1986 to 1994, economic growth has not been very different from one group to another. Over 10 years, however, 0.5 percent of difference between

Table 6: The Size of Government and Economic Performance in Different Country Groups, about 1990.

	Big Government	Medium Government	Small Government	Newly Industrialized Countries
Real GDP growth (1986-1994)	2.0	2.6	2.5	6.2
Standard deviation of GDP growth (1986-1994)	1.6	2.1	1.9	...
PPP-based per capita GNP (US$)	18,280	17,297	20,448	16,673
Gross fixed capital formation (in percent of GDP)	20.5	21.3	20.7	31.2
Inflation (1986-1994)	3.9	3.7	3.7	15.3
Public debt (in percent of GDP)	79.0	59.9	53.3	13.5
Economic freedom indicator (10 = best)	6.6	7.2	7.6	7.5
Size of shadow economy (in percent of GDP)	17.7	12.0	9.4	...

Sources: Gwartney, Lawson and Block (1996); OECD Economic Outlook (various); UN, Human Development Report (various); Schneider (1997).

small and big governments accumulates to more than 5 percent, which is not an insignificant amount. In addition, a growth rate of 2.5 percent versus 2 percent can make the crucial difference between declining or growing unemployment, as the growth of productivity and the labour force was in this order of magnitude in many industrialized countries in the past decade. Furthermore, GDP per capita is much higher in countries with small governments. In the 1960s and 1970s, in general the GDP per capita of poorer countries moved significantly closer to that of the richer countries. The fact that the GDP per capita of poorer countries with large public sectors has not been catching up to that of richer countries over the past 10 years could indicate an increasing adverse effect of large public sectors on growth.

It is also worth noting that GDP per capita (based on purchasing power parity) has been growing rapidly in the newly industrialized countries. In fact, all of these countries were catching up to the richer countries quickly. Hong Kong and Singapore show GDP per capita equal to some of the richest industrialized countries.

One of the main justifications for growing public spending since the Great Depression and the publication of Keynes's ideas has been the assumed need for a stabilization policy directed at reducing fluctuations in growth over the business cycle. However, countries with small governments rank in between countries with large and medium governments regarding the standard deviation of GDP growth. The ratio of the standard deviation and the average growth rate (the coefficient of variation) for countries with small governments is the lowest amongst the industrialized country groups. There is hence no evidence that higher public spending leads to more stable growth paths.

The next two indicators, formation of gross fixed capital and inflation, do not show much difference across groups of countries. This illustrates that large public spending has so far not undermined investors' confidence or monetary stability. However, public debt has been growing rapidly in the past two decades, particularly in countries with large public sectors. Public debt averages almost 80 percent of GDP in countries with big governments, and some of the most highly indebted industrial countries like Italy or Greece have been paying considerable risk premiums on their public debt obligations.[10] Note also that public debt in newly industrialized countries is very small, reflecting the low deficits that they have had.

In recent years, a number of other indicators measuring countries' economic health have been developed. One of them is the economic freedom indicator by James Gwartney, Robert Lawson and Walter Block (Gwartney, Lawson and Block 1996; Gwartney and Lawson 1997). Their composite index of economic freedom shows that countries with small governments and the newly industrialized countries perform very well on this score. The size of the shadow (or underground) economy is another indicator that reflects people's willingness to opt out of the formal economy. Schneider (1997) has provided estimates of the shadow economy for a number of industrialized countries. We can observe a strong correlation between high spending by government (and corresponding taxes) and the size of the shadow economy. One-sixth of the economies with big governments are estimated to be informal. This compares with an underground economy of less than one-tenth in countries with relatively small public sectors.

More details on small governments

So far we have compared various administrative, social, and economic indicators among groups of countries. We found that, on balance, small governments do not perform worse and often perform better than big governments in promoting social and economic well-being. This section will focus on a number of countries with relatively small governments. The basic positive message from above remains: good social and economic indicators are compatible with small public sectors. However, small governments do not perform equally well in all countries and in all areas.

Tables 7a and 7b compare various administrative, social, and economic indicators for 6 countries: the United States, Japan, Switzerland, Chile, Korea, and Singapore. Indicators of administrative efficiency show some variance among these countries. The indicators for Chile and Korea show relatively low scores for the efficiency of the judiciary while those for Japan and Korea are below average for red tape and corruption. Singapore and Switzerland, on the other hand, show perfect or near perfect scores in all three categories.

Japan, Switzerland, Korea, and Singapore, on balance, show the best scores for social and distributional indicators. There is not much difference among these countries in life expectancy, infant mortality, and secondary school enrollment. However, Korea has lower life expectancy, and Korea and Chile have slightly higher infant mortality, than the other countries. However, the United States also reports relatively high infant mortality. There seems to be a considerable difference in the availability and quality of education. Japan, Korea, and to a somewhat lesser extent Switzerland report educational achievements for secondary school students much above the average for industrial countries, whereas secondary education in the United States ranks below average. We do not have data on educational attainment for Chile but its secondary school enrollment rate is relatively low. Furthermore, Chile reports a relatively unequal income distribution. The poorest 40 percent of households receive about 10 percent of national income—half as much as they do in Korea. If we added indicators of social stability such as the divorce rate or the share of the population in prison, the United States would look relatively unfavorable. While it is questionable whether this is the result of too little social welfare spending, the social indicators show nevertheless that American social policies do not always secure high quality secondary education, and seem to be less effective in preventing violence than in many other industrialized countries.

Table 7a illustrates the low unemployment rates in industrialized countries with small public sectors and table 7b shows the rates in newly industrialized countries. The figures contrast with those for western Europe, where many countries report double-digit unemployment. All 6 countries report full or near full-employment. However, it is worth remembering that Korea's and Singapore's jobless rate below three percent was typical for many industrialized countries during the 1960s as well.

Table 7a: Indicators of government performance for selected industrialized countries with "small" governments (early 1990s)

	United States	Japan	Switzerland
Administrative efficiency indicators:[2]			
Efficiency of Judiciary system	10.0	10.0	10.0
Red tape	9.3	8.5	10.0
Corruption	7.8	6.7	8.8
Social and distributional indicators:			
Life expectancy (1995)	77	80	78
Infant mortality (per 1,000 live births, 1995)	8	4	6
Secondary school enrolment ratio	97	96	91
Average achievement in mathematics (8th grade, 1994)	500	605	545
Income share of lowest 40% of households (about 1990)	15.4	17.7	18.7
Labour market indicators:			
Unemployment (mid 1990s)	5.4	3.3	4.7
Economic Indicators:			
Economic growth (%, 1991-1995)	2.3	1.3	1.6
PPP-based per capita GNP (US$, 1995)	26,980	22,110	25,860
Inflation (1991-1995)	3.2	1.4	3.2
Gross public debt (1994/1995)	64.3	81.3	48.2
Economic and political freedom indicators:[2]			
Economic freedom	8.0	7.3	7.9
Political rights	10.0	10.0	10.0
Civil liberties	10.0	10.0	10.0

Sources: See previous Tables 2, 3 and 6.
[1] External debt only.
[2] Ranking between 0 = worst and 10 = best.

Table 7b: Indicators of government performance for selected newly industrialized countries (early 1990s)

	Chile	Korea	Singapore
Administrative efficiency indicators:[2]			
Efficiency of Judiciary system	7.3	6.0	10.0
Red tape	9.3	6.5	10.0
Corruption	7.9	4.3	9.3
Social and distributional indicators:			
Life expectancy (1995)	76	72	77
Infant mortality (per 1,000 live births, 1995)	12	10	4
Secondary school enrolment ratio	70	93	84
Average achievement in mathematics (8th grade, 1994)	...	607	...
Income share of lowest 40% of households (about 1990)	10.5	19.7	17.3
Labour market indicators:			
Unemployment (mid 1990s)	4.6	2.4	2.7
Economic Indicators:			
Economic growth (%, 1991-1995)	7.4	9.5	8.8
PPP-based per capita GNP (US$, 1995)	9,520	11,450	22,770
Inflation (1991-1995)	13.9	6.2	2.5
Gross public debt (1994/1995)	17.4[1]	8.0	15.2
Economic and political freedom indicators:[2]			
Economic freedom	6.2	6.7	8.2
Political rights	7.0	9.0	7.0
Civil liberties	8.0	8.0	7.0

Economic growth across these 6 countries with small public sectors also provides an interesting picture. The United States and the three newly industrialized countries show relatively high growth in the early 1990s. The Asian crisis, however, has somewhat tarnished this picture. Japan and Switzerland report only very sluggish economic growth during the first half of the 1990s. This could be due to the fact that these countries have many regulations (like price regulations or cartels) that do not burden the budget but do constrain economic growth.[11]

GDP per capita (based on purchasing power parity) in the three industrialized countries and Singapore is among the highest in the world. Chile and Korea have been catching up rapidly but still lag considerably behind. Another period of rapid growth, however, may see them catch up with some of the poorer industrial countries like Ireland, New Zealand and Spain. Inflation has also been very low in these countries and public debt is relatively low. The United States and Switzerland show public debt near the average for small governments; only Japan reports a considerable burden of public debt. However, on a "net" basis, Japan's public debt is also relatively small.

Towards smaller government and government reform

A considerable body of literature has emerged in recent years discussing government performance and reform (see Tanzi and Schuknecht 1998 and 1997b). Various studies discuss the private versus public provision of goods and services and social security and the role of budgetary institutions in maintaining small and efficient governments with low fiscal deficits.[12] The conclusion of this debate seems to be that governments could introduce considerable changes to the way they are currently doing things.

A number of countries such as New Zealand or Chile have introduced fundamental fiscal and economic reforms to cut back the role and size of government in the economy. Some other industrialized countries such as Australia, Belgium, Ireland, the Netherlands, the United Kingdom, and, more recently, Italy and Canada have started reforming their institutions, cutting public spending, and reducing their large fiscal deficits. Newly industrialized and developing countries like Argentina, Malaysia, and Mauritius have introduced far-reaching public sector reforms as well. Privatization of public enterprises and services, and social-security reform with fully funded pension systems are reported for a number of these countries. There is also renewed interest in rules limiting fiscal deficits. The Maastricht Treaty of 1991 established strict fiscal eligibility criteria for the members of European Monetary Union (EMU) and many countries in the European Union (EU) have been reducing their fiscal deficits in the run-up to EMU. The EU members have also agreed on the so-called "stability and growth pact" limiting budget deficits after the introduction of the Euro. Meanwhile, the United States had committed itself to achieving a balanced budget by the year 2002 but it expects to report a surplus in the fiscal year 1998.

Some of these countries have experienced higher growth and falling unemployment as a result of reform. However, in some cases reforms can take a number of years to become credible and show the desired results.[13] Furthermore, many industrialized countries have yet to tackle their high spending levels and the upward trend in spending that results from generous welfare programs especially.

The purpose of this chapter was to show that countries can achieve reasonable social and economic performance indicators without their governments absorbing over 40 or 50 percent of GDP. The newly industrialized countries with public spending of about 20 percent of GDP or the industrialized countries with government expenditure of 30 percent or not more than 40 percent of GDP might provide some useful lessons for the other countries with higher levels of public spending. Although 30 percent of GDP of public spending may be a useful benchmark for some countries trying to curtail their public sectors, this does not mean that it is the optimal size of government. This depends very much on the circumstances of each country, the efficiency of countries' public sectors, and the preferences of their populations. Nevertheless, given the growing interest in reducing public spending and implementing government reforms, we can repeat our previous optimistic forecast (Tanzi and Schuknecht 1998) that we are likely to see somewhat smaller and more efficient governments in the future.

Notes

1 For a survey of the change in economic ideas and how it affected institutions and policies see, for example, Tanzi and Schuknecht 1998 and 1997a.
2 For one of the less populist studies promoting this view, see Rodrick 1997.
3 In fact, Keynes in correspondence with Colin Clark confirmed the latter's suggestion that "25 percent [of GDP] is probably near the maximum tolerable proportion of taxation" (Clark 1964).
4 This is the same methodology followed in Tanzi and Schuknecht 1997a.
5 In some countries, part or all health expenditure is financed through the social security system and education is financed, in part, through grants to private schools. These expenditures are then accounted under transfers and subsidies and not under public consumption.

6 The data on the income share of the poorest quintile is often not very reliable.
7 The relatively poor targeting of public expenditure in many Latin American countries is discussed in Tanzi 1996.
8 These findings are consistent with the findings for developing and industrialized countries by Bourguignon and Morrisson 1983 and 1990.
9 High social-security benefits may reduce the efforts to look for work but labour market rigidities are also very important (if not more important) in explaining high unemployment in many countries (Lindbeck 1996).
10 Italy, in particular, has undertaken major efforts at fiscal consolidation in preparation for European Monetary Union. The risk premium on its public debt therefore declined considerably in the mid-1990s.
11 Tanzi 1995 discusses the dangers of replacing budgetary policies with less efficient quasi-fiscal regulations.
12 For a more detailed study of budgetary institutions see Milesi-Feretti 1996; for a study of private versus public provision of goods and services, see Mueller 1989. On pension reform, see, *e.g.*, World Bank 1994.
13 More rapid positive responses are possible under certain circumstances (see Giavazzi and Pagano 1990; Alesina and Perotti 1995b; McDermott and Wescott 1996) and the examples of Ireland and Denmark are often mentioned in this context. Interestingly enough, the Italian economy has been growing considerably while the fiscal deficit was cut by an extraordinary 4 percent in 1997.

Bibliography

Alesina, Alberto, and Roberto Perotti (1995a) Political Economy of Budget Deficits. *International Monetary Fund Staff Papers* 42,1 (March): 1–31.
———— (1995b) *Fiscal Expansion and Fiscal Adjustment in OECD Countries.* NBER Working Paper No. 5214.
Altenstetter, Christa (1986) German Social Security Programs: An Interpretation of their Development, 1883-1985. In Douglas E. Ashford and E.W. Kelley (eds.), *Nationalizing Social Security in Europe and America* (Greenwich, CT: JAI Press): 73–97.
Bourguignon, F., and C. Morrison (1983). The Level of World Inequality: How Much Can One Say? *Review of Income and Wealth*: 217–41.
———— (1990). Income Distribution, Development and Foreign Trade. *European Economic Review* 34: 1113–32.
Buchanan, James M., Charles K. Rowley, and Robert D. Tollison, eds. (1987). *Deficits.* New York: Basil Blackwell.
Clark, Colin (1964). *Taxmanship.* Hobart paper 26. Institute of Economic Affairs.
Connell, W.F. (1980). *A History of Education in the Twentieth Century World.* New York: Teachers College Press.

Flora, Peter, Kraus, Franz, and Winfried Pfennig (1987). *State, Economy and Society in Western Europe, 1815–1975*. Chicago: St. James Press.

Forte, Francesco, and Alan T. Peacock (1985). *Public Expenditure and Government Growth*. Oxford: Basil Blackwell.

Galbraith, John Kenneth (1958). *The Affluent Society*. Boston: Houghton Mifflin.

Giavazzi, Francesco, and Marco Pagano (1990). Can Severe Fiscal Contractions Be Expansionary? Tales of Two Small European Countries. *NBER Working Paper No 3372*.

Gwartney, James D., and Richard Lawson (1997). *Economic Freedom of the World: 1997 Annual Report*. Vancouver, BC: The Fraser Institute.

Gwartney, James D., Richard Lawson, and Walter Block (1996). *Economic Freedom of the World, 1975–1995*. Vancouver, BC: The Fraser Institute.

International Monetary Fund (1996). *Government Finance Statistics Yearbook* (GFS). Washington, DC: International Monetary Fund.

Keynes, John Maynard (1936). *The General Theory of Employment, Interest, and Money*. (San Diego, CA: Harcourt Bruce Janovich.

Leroy-Beaulieu, Paul (1988). *Traité de la Science des Finances*. Paris: Guillaumin.

Lindbeck, Assar (1996). The West European Employment Problem. *Weltwirtschaflltiches Archiv* 132, 4: 609–37.

Mauro, Paolo (1995). Corruption and Growth. *Quarterly Journal of Economics* 110: 681–712.

McDermott, John, and Robert Wescott (1996). *An Empirical Analysis of Fiscal Adjustments*. IMF Working Paper WP/96/59. Washington, DC: International Monetary Fund.

Milesi-Feretti, Gian-Maria (1996). *Fiscal Rules and the Budget Process*. IMF Working Paper WP/96/60. Washington, DC: International Monetary Fund.

Mitchell, B.R. (1995). *International Historical Statistics: Africa, Asia and Oceania, 1750–1988*. 2nd rev. ed. New York: Stockton Press.

Moser, Peter (1994). Constitutional Protection of Economic Rights: The Swiss and U.S. Experience in Comparison. *Constitutional Political Economy* 5: 61–79.

Mueller, Dennis C. (1986). *The Growth of Government: A Public Choice Perspective*. DM/86/33. Washington, DC: International Monetary Fund.

——— (1989). *Public Choice II*. Cambridge: Cambridge University Press.

Musgrave, Richard A. (1959). *The Theory of Public Finance: A Study in Public Economy*. New York: McGraw-Hill.

Organisation for Economic Cooperation and Development [OECD] (1995). *Income Distribution in OECD Countries*. Paris: OECD.

——— 1996. *Education at a Glance*. Paris: OECD.

——— (various). *OECD Economic Outlook*. Paris: OECD.

Palda, Filip (1997). Fiscal Churning and Political Efficiency. *Kyklos* 50: 189–206.

Peacock, Alan, and Jack Wiseman (1961). *The Growth of Public Expenditure in the United Kingdom*. Princeton: Princeton University Press.

Rodrik, Dani (1997). *Has Globalization Gone Too Far?* Washington, DC: Institute for International Economics.

Schneider, Friedrich (1997) Empirical Results for the Size of the Shadow Economy of Western European Countries Over Time. Unpublished paper. University of Linz.

Tanzi, Vito (1986). Public Expenditure and Public Debt. In John Bristow and Declan McDonagh (eds.), *Public Expenditure: The Key Issues* (Dublin: Institute of Public Administration): 6–37.

———— (1995). *Government Role and the Efficiency of Policy Instruments*. IMF Working Paper WP/95/100. Washington, DC: International Monetary Fund.

———— (1996). Fiscal Policy and Income Distribution. Paper presented at the Conference on Economic Growth and Equity: International Experience and Policies, July 12/13, 1996, Santiago, Chile

Tanzi, Vito and Ludger Schuknecht (1998). *The Growth of Government and the Reform of the State in Industrial Countries*. In Andres Solimano (ed.), *Social Inequality* (Ann Arbor, MI: Michigan University Press.

———— (1997a). Reconsidering the Fiscal Role of Government: The International Perspective. *American Economic Review* 87: 164–68.

———— (1997b). Reforming Government: An Overview over the Recent Experience. *European Journal of Political Economy* 13: 395–417.

Transparency International (1996). *Report 1996*. Berlin: Transparency International.

United Nations Development Program (various). *Human Development Report*. New York: Oxford University Press.

World Bank (1994). *Averting the Old Age Crisis: Policies to Protect the Old and Promote Growth*. New York: Oxford University Press.

———— (1997). *World Development Indicators*. Washington DC: The World Bank.

Zandvakili, Sourushe (1994). Income Distribution and Redistribution through Taxation: An International Comparison. *Empirical Economics* 19, 3: 473–91.

The Underground Economy
Minimizing the Size of Government

David E.A. Giles

This chapter discusses several aspects of work that has been undertaken by the author, over the past three years, to measure the extent of the "hidden economy" (HE) in New Zealand; to explore some of its determinants, and its responsiveness to fiscal instruments; and to investigate the size of the associated "tax gap" in that country. The work on which I draw has been discussed in more detail, and in somewhat more technical terms, in Giles 1997a, 1997b, 1997c, 1997d, 1997e, 1998, for example, and in Caragata and Giles 1996 and Giles and Caragata 1996. This work, which was commissioned by the New Zealand Inland Revenue Department, formed part of a much broader research program into many aspects of taxation policy. The principal findings of that research are reported in Caragata 1998b.

In this paper, we outline the results of some extensive econometric modeling that has been undertaken to establish a time-series of the size of New Zealand's hidden economy from 1968 to 1994. The derivation of these data has facilitated a good deal of associated research and here we will be drawing on those findings to comment, in particular, on the relationship between the hidden economy and taxation policy, in terms both of the overall tax burden and also of the nature of the "tax mix" between, for example, direct and indirect taxes and so on. Our research in this area has revealed a clear and statistically significant link between high taxes and the size of the underground economy. Moreover, we have been able to establish the extent to which reductions in the tax burden, and changes to its "mix," can lower illicit activity in the economy. Interestingly, and very importantly, this in turn enables us to establish an "optimal" aggregate tax rate, if the objective is to maximize the impact on the HE. Many of the broad lessons that emerge from this research have applicability in the Canadian context, and more specific work of this type with Canadian data is currently being undertaken by the author and colleagues.

The plan of the rest of the paper is as follows. Section 1 provides some brief summary information about general international trends in the size of the HE. These trends are drawn from a variety of empirical studies on the subject. More specific evidence about the size and nature of the HE, and about the associated tax gap in New Zealand is discussed in section 2. Section 3 discusses some of the key features of the tax-responsiveness of the HE that emerged from our research for New Zealand; and the section 4 explores a few very tentative lessons that can be drawn for the Canadian economy from this evidence.

The international face of the hidden economy

Considerable empirical research has been undertaken in a very wide range of countries, and employing various techniques, in an attempt to obtain measures of the magnitude of the underground economy. These measures generally provide somewhat varied evidence. For example, Frey and Weck-Hanneman (1984) report that for 17 countries from the Organisation for Economic Cooperation and Development (OECD) in 1978, the size of the HE (as a percentage of GNP) varied from 4.1 percent for Japan, 8.0 percent for the United Kingdom, 8.3 percent for the United States, to 13.2 percent in the case of Sweden. Canada was assessed at the sample mean of 8.8 percent, a figure that should be compared with the 5 percent to 7 percent of GDP that Mirus and Smith (1994) estimated for Canada in 1976, and the 15 percent that they estimated for 1990. Spiro (1993) estimated the Canadian underground economy at between 8 percent and 11 percent of GDP in 1993, and other Canadian (and international) evidence may be found in the various papers in Lippert and Walker (1997). By way of summarizing the various empirical studies for Canada, Mirus and Smith conclude that "a number of studies suggest significant growth and an order of magnitude of 12 to 15 percent of GDP for Canada's underground economy when we include illegal activities but exclude barter-based transactions which our definition says should be counted" (1997: 8).

Evidence from the United States in 1970 yields a range, for the ratio of the HE to GDP, from 2.6 percent (Tanzi 1983) to 11 percent

(Schneider and Pommerehne 1985), while other studies summarized by Aigner *et al.* (1988) report American figures in 1978 that range from 4 percent (Park 1979) to 33 percent (Feige 1982) of GNP. In contrast, Bhattacharyya (1990) estimates the HE for the United Kingdom to be 3.8 percent of GNP in 1960, peaking at 11.1 percent in 1976, and averaging about 8 percent in 1984; while a British Inland Revenue analysis reported by Chote (1995) suggests that the HE may be 6 percent to 8 percent of GDP. Schneider (1997) provides some recent comparative information for a wide range of countries, some of which is summarized in figure 1, together with the earlier (and comparable) results of Frey and Weck-Hannemann (1984).

There are also several surveys of the literature on measuring the Hidden Economy, including those of Blades (1982), Boeschoten and Fase (1984), Frey and Pommerehne (1982, 1984), Gaertner and Wenig (1985), Kirchgaessner (1984) and Weck (1983). These studies can be grouped loosely in the following way.

(1) *Tax Evasion:* It may be possible to use surveys relating to taxation compliance or tax-audit data to obtain estimates of underground activity (*e.g.* Isachsen *et al.* 1982; Morgensen 1985; Giles 1997e). Though this approach generally under-estimates the size of the HE, it does provide a profile of the underground labour force.

(2) *National Income and Expenditure:* A positive "initial discrepancy" between the expenditure and income estimates of GNP may reflect hidden activity (*e.g.* Macafee 1980; Park 1979). However, this approach is rather crude as such a discrepancy can be just the cumulation of various measurement errors.

(3) *Labour Force Participation Rates:* Contini (1981), Fuà (1976) and others have estimated the size of the HE from changes in the labour force participation rate. A decline in this rate over time or a low rate relative to those in comparable economies may reflect a movement of the workforce from the measured economy into hidden activities. One weakness of this approach is that many participants in the HE also work in the measured economy, so an *under-estimation* of unrecorded output is likely. Tedds, in her structural modeling of the Canadian HE (1998), takes account of multiple job-holdings.

(4) *Currency Demand:* Changes in the size of the HE can be judged from movements in the demand for currency, *i.e.* notes and coins in circulation (see, *e.g.*, Tanzi 1980 and Spiro 1993). The "transactions approach" (*e.g.* Feige 1979) infers the size of overall economic activity from the total quantity of money. The difference between this inferred activity and observed economic activity measures the extent of the HE. There are

Figure 1: Size of the hidden economy as percent of GDP

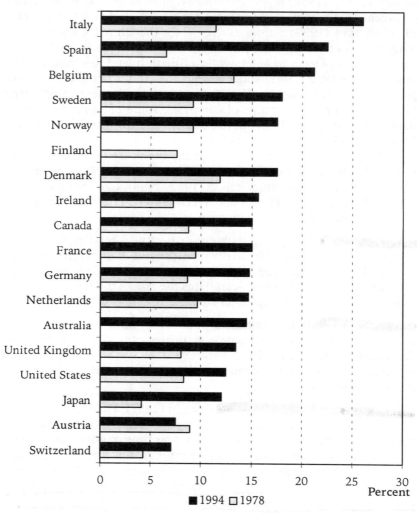

Source: Frey and Weck-Hannemann 1984; Schneider 1997.

weaknesses with this approach too, including the need for accurate measures of the total volume of transactions and an assumption of a constant transactions ratio. Other currency-demand approaches to measuring the HE include adding tax rate variables to the demand equations (*e.g.* Cagan 1958 for the United States; Macecish 1962 for Canada) or allowing for differential velocities of circulation in the measured and hidden sectors (*e.g.* Bhattacharyya 1990 for the United Kingdom).

(5) *Latent Variable Models:* The approaches above focus on just *one* cause of underground economic activity and one indicator. Frey and Weck-Hannemann (1984) and Aigner *et al.* (1988) use "latent variable" structural modeling to measure the size of the Hidden Economy. The (unobservable) latent variable here is the extent of underground activity, perhaps expressed as a percentage of measured real GDP. The MIMIC (Multiple Indicators, Multiple Causes) model of Zellner (1970), Goldberger (1972), Jöreskog and Goldberger (1975), and Jöreskog and Sörbom (1993) allows for *several* "indicator" variables and *several* "causal" variables in forming structural relationships to "explain" the latent variable(s). This approach using the latent variable / MIMIC model is the basis for our own analysis of the HE in New Zealand, the full technical details of which are given by Giles 1997a.

Given the variety of estimation methods that have been used to measure the size of the HE, it is not surprising that the results show wide variations across countries and over time. However, when we concentrate on one or two of the more comprehensive methods, and fair comparisons are made with comparable data across different countries for a specific time-period, some interesting patterns emerge. As can be seen in figure 1, the average HE in countries belonging to the OECD seems to be about 15 percent of GDP; The HE in Canada seems to be of typical size, at least on the basis of the evidence to date. Further, *in percentage terms,* the size of the HE has grown over past 20 years. Schneider's (1997) figures suggest that it has tripled since the 1960s. Figure 2 illustrates the variation among measures of the size of the Canadian HE, depending on the method and data used.

Why has *relative size* of the HE apparently grown over time in virtually every country where such studies have been undertaken? (Clearly, there are several answers to this question and a useful discussion may be found in Caragata 1998a: 71–76.) One fact is plain: in almost all of these countries the overall tax burden as measured in terms of the *effective tax rate* (the ratio of tax revenue to GDP, say) has grown. This is very clear when one inspects the OECD's data constructed on a comparable basis. (The latest year for which this comparison can be made is currently 1994.) Figure 3 illustrates this point for Canada and New Zealand, which both had very similar effective tax rates in 1994 even though, as described below, their *statutory tax rate* systems are vastly different. Canada's effective tax rate was 36.1 percent (an increase of 15.3 percent over the period shown); New Zealand's was 37.0 percent (an increase of 35.0 percent); and the OECD average was 38.4 percent (an increase of 30.2 percent).

In some cases, the tax system has also grown more complex, making it more difficult for some tax-payers to comply. In New Zealand,

Figure 2: Canadian hidden economy as percent of GDP

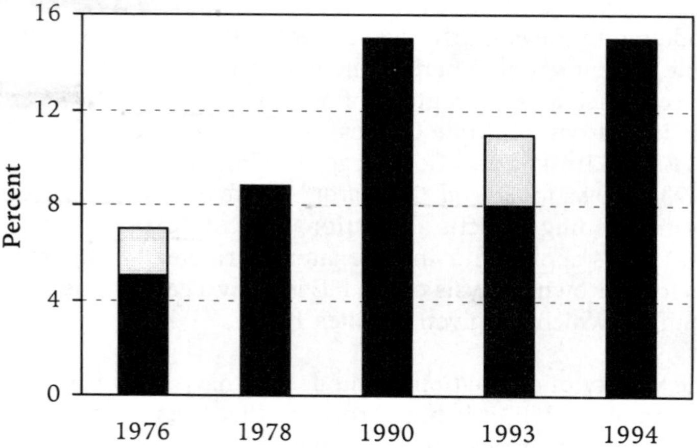

Source: Various authors. Note: Stacked bars denote a range.

however, just the opposite is true. Some of the tax-related highlights of the fiscal reforms in that country included the following:

(1) *October 1986*: Introduction of the GST at a rate of 10 percent, with no exceptions, and written into the marked prices of retail goods. Simultaneously, wholesale taxes (which had been up to 20 percent) were abolished; the five-step (20 percent to 60 percent, plus a 10 percent surcharge) personal statutory tax scale was simplified to a three-step scale: 15 percent, 30 percent, 48 percent.

(2) *1987 Budget*: A single, flat, personal statutory tax rate was proposed but not implemented.

(3) *1988 Budget*: The company tax rate was reduced from 45 percent to 28 percent, and the personal tax scale was simplified to two steps, with marginal rates of 24 percent and 33 percent.

(4) *1989 Budget*: The land tax rate was reduced from 2 percent to 1 percent, the GST rate was raised to 12.5 percent from 1 July 1989, and the company tax was raised to 33 percent from 1 April 1989.

(5) *1990 Budget*: Excise taxes on automobiles and land taxes were abolished, and the GST threshold was raised from NZ$24,000 to NZ$30,000.

(6) *1991 Budget*: There were various major international tax and company tax reforms.

Figure 3: Ratio of total tax to GDP (including local taxes)

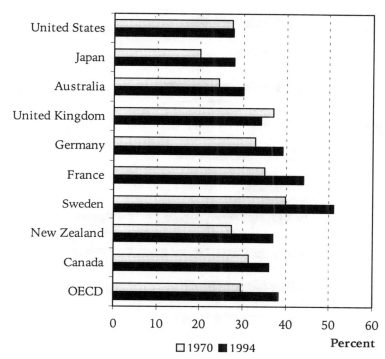

□ 1970 ■ 1994   **Percent**

Source: Caragata 1998b.

(7) *1996 Budget*: Reductions were made to the personal income tax rates, making them 21.5 percent on the first NZ$34,200 and 33 percent on income above that.

(8) *1997 Budget*: From 1 July 1998, personal income taxes are to be reduced to 19.5 percent on the first NZ$38,000, and 33 percent on income above that.

Another important factor affecting the size of the HE appears to be the tax-mix. As can be seen in figure 4, the ratio of revenue from *personal* income taxes to GDP has changed in different ways in different countries between 1980 and 1994. In Canada, it increased by 24.1 percent to reach 13.4 percent in the mid-1990s. In New Zealand, by contrast, this ratio *fell* by 18.2 percent to a value of 16.6 percent in 1994. Some of the reasons for this will be made clear below. Overall, for OECD countries, the effective personal income tax rate was 12.4 percent in

Figure 4: Ratio of personal tax to GDP

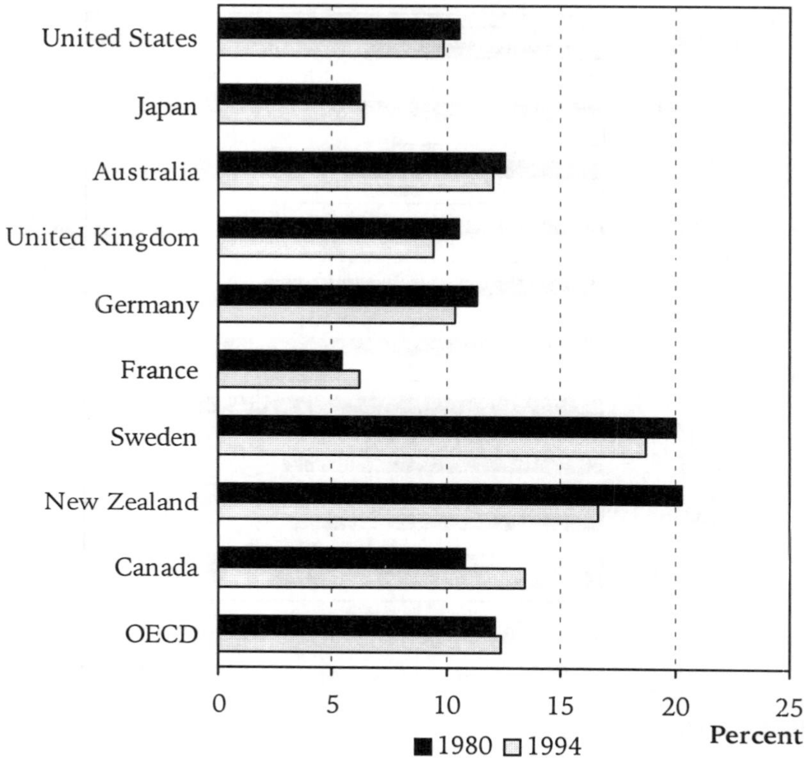

Source: Caragata 1998b.

1994, up just 2.5 percent since 1980. The case of New Zealand is interesting, especially given the economic reforms in that country since early 1984. Figures 5 and 6, which exclude taxes imposed by local
authorities provide a useful overview (if these taxes are *included*, then
the tax burden in New Zealand is at its highest point in 100 years). We
see that there has been a decline in personal taxes since the 1980s, and
an increase in indirect taxes since the mid-1970s.

Greater regulation of labour and product markets is also a factor
that is generally regarded as driving the HE, though again this influence
has been on the decline in New Zealand (though not significantly so in
Canada) since the mid 1980s. On the other hand, the growing trends
in the international labour market towards more self-employment and
more multiple (part-time) jobs together with the growing rates of

Figure 5: Ratio of tax to GDP in New Zealand

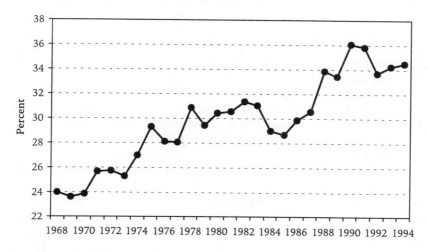

Source: Giles and Caragata 1996.

bankruptcy and of fraud and related criminal activities that have been documented for many countries are consistent with an expanding informal sector in the economy.

Figure 6: Shares of total tax in New Zealand

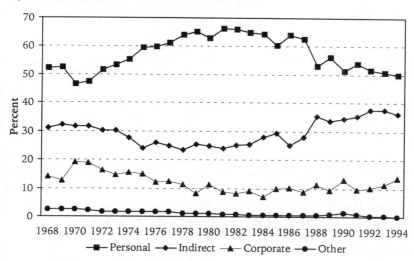

Source: Caragata and Giles 1996.

New Zealand's hidden economy and tax gap

Since 1995 we have been developing econometric models of the aggregate size of the HE in New Zealand and the changes in such activity since the late 1960s. To do this, we have developed some new modeling techniques, including combining the estimation of a currency-demand equation that allows for both hidden and measured activity in a novel way, with the estimation of a MIMIC model.

This work comprises the first empirical investigation of the HE in that country and is more comprehensive than most similar studies for other countries. In particular, it employs novel data for regulatory effects and detailed taxation data. There appears to be no other research into this problem that combines both of the above types of models and none that takes explicit account of the non-stationarity of the time-series data in an appropriate manner. More recently, we have also corroborated our macro-level time-series estimates by analyzing cross-sectional data based on the tax-audit records for individual firms (see Giles 1997f). The central part of our modeling involves the estimation of a structural MIMIC model in which the HE is a latent variable. By using a range of measurable indicator variables and causal variables (see table 1), we are able to generate a predicted annual time-path for the HE from 1968 to 1994.

Table 1: Variables used in hidden-economy model

Indicators	Causes
Real GDP growth	Average and marginal tax rates; GST and self-employed tax
Ratio of currency to money supply	Unemployment rate; inflation rate; real disposable income
Male participation in labour force	Size of public sector; indices of economic regulation

The details of this technique, of the results, and of the associated diagnostic testing of the model are reported in Giles 1997a, and the estimated HE time-series appears in figure 7. As it has in a wide range of countries (figure 1), the HE in New Zealand has been growing over time relative to GDP, ranging from 6.8 percent in 1968 to 11.3 percent in 1994, and averaging 8.8 percent over the period shown. As figure 8 illustrates, hidden output also appears to be more volatile than measured

Figure 7: New Zealand's hidden economy as percent of GDP

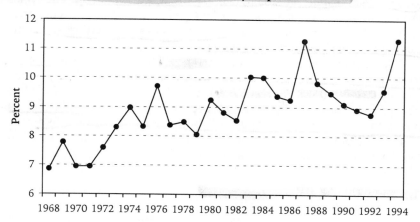

Source: Giles 1997a.

Figure 8: Measured and hidden GDP in New Zealand
(in millions of real 1982/83 dollars)

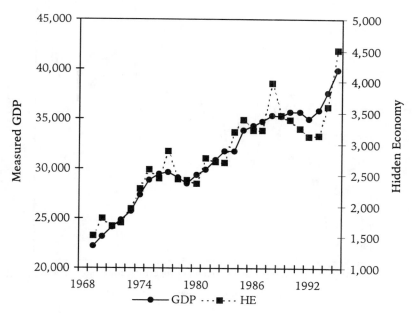

Source: Giles 1997a.

GDP. Giles (1997b) has established that there is a significant (Granger-) causal effect *from* measured GDP *to* the HE but not *vice versa*. The cycles in both of these series are shown by Giles to be relatively symmetric (1997c, 1998), and Giles has also shown that tax-related prosecutions can have a significant effect on the HE (1997d).

We can compute the size of the tax gap (*i.e.* the proportion of *potential* tax revenue that is foregone as a result of hidden activity) as: tax gap = (tax revenue × (HE/GDP)) and the results of this for New Zealand are shown in figure 9. We see that the tax gap rose from 6.4 percent to 10.2 percent of total tax liability between 1968 to 1994; that is, it rose from 1.6 percent to 4.0 percent of GDP, or from NZ$0.1 billion to NZ$3.2 billion in nominal terms. By way of comparison, Inter-

Figure 9: The tax gap in New Zealand

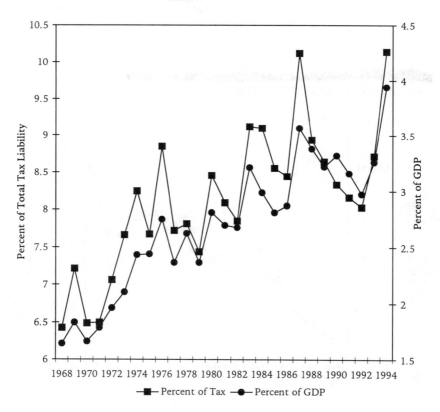

Source: Giles 1997a.

nal Revenue Service (1996) data for the United States suggests tax gaps of 19 percent (1985), 18 percent (1988), and 17 percent (1992) of total tax liability for individual tax-payers. The figure of 10.2 percent for New Zealand in 1994 is supported by the tax-audit figures for firms analyzed by Giles (1997e), which suggest a tax gap of the order of 10.8 percent for these economic units during the period from 1993 to 1995.

A little casual empiricism for the Canadian situation is also interesting here. Suppose we were to take 15 percent of GDP as the consensus of the research discussed in section 1 for the size of the HE in 1994. The ration of tax to GDP was 36.1 percent in that year, which implies a tax gap of about 5.4 percent of GDP. Nominal GDP was CDN$654.8 billion in 1994 and total tax revenue was CDN$236.4 billion; *this would imply a tax gap of CDN$35.5 billion, or 13.1 percent of total tax liability.*

The responsiveness of the hidden economy to taxes

In section 2, we noted some important patterns and trends in both the aggregate tax burden and the tax mix in New Zealand and other countries in recent years. Our own work (much of which is summarized in Caragata 1998a and 1998b) and that of several other authors from other countries supports the view that the chief causes of underground activity and tax-evasion include high and rising tax burdens, inflation, rising real disposable incomes, and declines in ethical standards. The link between the tax burden and the relative size of the HE in New Zealand has been explored by means of extensive simulations by Giles and Caragata (1996). Their results show that there is clear positive causality *from* Tax Revenue/GDP *to* HE/GDP and that, on average over their sample, just over one-half of the HE is "hard-core"—*i.e.* unresponsive to changes in taxation policy. Even in the limit when Tax Revenue/GDP = 0, the size of the HE is still 4.7 percent of GDP.

They find that the split between hard-core and soft-core hidden economic activity varies over the business cycle; hard-core tax evasion increases, relatively, during cyclical troughs. For example, they estimated 65 percent of evasion to be hard core in 1968 but only 39 percent in 1994. In the latter case, this meant that the hard core evasion amounted to 5.1 percent of GDP and implied a tax loss of NZ$1.2 billion. By way of support, the micro-evidence from the tax-audit records analyzed by Giles (1997e) indicates an extrapolated figure for a hard-core HE equivalent to 5 percent of GDP. The other NZ$2 billion of the tax gap in 1994 was, therefore, apparently tax-sensitive. Giles and Caragata (1996) also show that successive reductions in the effective tax rate will reduce the ratio HE/GDP, though not uniformly.

The elasticity between these two ratios increases with the tax burden, a unit elasticity apparently arising at an effective tax rate of 47 percent. Table 2, part (a), provides some details for the average responses over the period from 1969 to 1994.

More specifically, in 1994 a 10 percent (*not* a 10 percentage-point) cut in the effective tax rate implies a 7.6 percent cut in the HE/GDP ratio. So, it is estimated that reducing the tax burden from 34.5 percent to 31.1 percent of GDP in New Zealand that year would have reduced the HE ratio from 11.3 percent to 10.4 percent of measured GDP. Recalling figure 6, it is also interesting to ask what would be the corresponding effects of changes in the tax mix? This is addressed (with or without changes to the overall tax burden) in further simulation work reported by Caragata and Giles (1996). They show that an increase in indirect taxes relative to direct taxes reduces the size of the HE/GDP ratio. Again, some illustrative average figures are given in table 2, part (b). There, the overall tax burden has been held constant by interchanging the shares of personal and indirect taxes, as shown in figure 6, year by year. Comparing tax burden and tax-mix effects, Caragata and Giles show that reductions in the former can have more impact than even quite substantial changes in the tax-mix. For instance, on the basis of the 1994 figures, a 10 percent uniform reduction in the tax burden is predicted to have the same effect as the rather dramatic policy change of interchanging the personal and indirect tax proportions of total tax. Perhaps the most striking implications of these simulations are that the impact of tax changes on the HE starts to decelerate at an effective tax rate of around 21 percent of GDP; and that combining tax cuts with a change towards relatively more indirect taxes enhances the reduction of the (HE/GDP) ratio.

Table 2: Simulated values for percent (HE/GDP) (average, 1969–1994)

		Percent reductions in ratio tax/GDP				
"Actual" %	0	20	40	60	80	100
(a) No Change in Tax Mix						
8.96	8.96	7.87	6.91	6.06	5.32	4.67
(b) Personal and Indirect Tax Rates Interchanged						
8.96	7.96	7.16	6.43	5.78	5.19	4.67

Some lessons for the Canadian situation

Although there is no definitive way to measure the size of the HE, we are now developing more sophisticated and reliable procedures for doing so, and the modeling that underlies the preceding discussion of underground activity in New Zealand is now being applied with Canadian data by the author and others (Tedds 1998). The tentative results to date clearly support the international evidence that the relative size of the HE has been growing over the past two or three decades. It is also clear from this evidence that the extent of the tax burden is a major driving force for the HE, and that the nature of the tax-mix also matters.

As far as the actual magnitude of the HE is concerned, the evidence for Canada is varied. Tax compliance in Canada, however, seems to be around the OECD average, suggesting underground activity of the order of about 15 percent of GDP in recent years. Of course, this is only a convenient way of stating this measure for comparative purposes—it does *not* imply that the official figures for Canada's GDP should be adjusted upwards by 15 percent to compensate for the HE, because many of the associated activities fall outside the definition of GDP. However, on the basis of this figure of 15 percent, there may be a tax gap of approximately CDN$35 billion in Canada.

Judging by the evidence from New Zealand, and using the response rates calculated by Giles and Caragata (1996), reducing the Canadian effective tax rate from 36.1 percent to 30 percent (which, interestingly, is that of Australia) would probably reduce the HE ratio from about 15 percent of GDP to about 13 percent. Ignoring the stimulation to economic growth, and other dynamic effects (which undoubtedly are significant, but are as yet unexplored), the tax gap would then fall from 5.4 percent of GDP to 3.9 percent of GDP; or from CDN$35.5 billion to about CDN$25.5 billion. If the role of government could be reduced even further, so that the Canadian effective tax rate were brought down to 21 percent—the optimal rate calculated for New Zealand by Caragata and Giles (1996)—the HE ratio might fall to 10 percent of GDP and the tax gap could fall to 2.1 percent of GDP or CDN$13.8 billion.

These figures are tentative, of course, but work that is currently in progress will enable us to provide more definitive measures shortly. In the meantime, the detailed empirical work with the New Zealand data provides us with some very important messages regarding the connection between the size of government, high effective tax rates, and the magnitude of the informal economy. Regardless of their precise numerical details, these are lessons that no policy-maker can afford to ignore.

References

Aigner, D.J., F. Schneider, and D. Ghosh (1988). Me and My Shadow: Estimating the Size of the Hidden Economy From Time Series Data. In W.A. Barnett *et al.* (eds.), *Dynamic Econometrics Modeling: Proceedings of the Third International Symposium in Economic Theory and Econometrics* (Cambridge: Cambridge University Press): 297–334.

Bhattacharyya, D.K. (1990). An Econometric Method of Estimating the "Hidden Economy," United Kingdom (1960–1984): Estimates and Tests. *Economic Journal* 100: 703–17.

Blades, D. (1982). *The Hidden Economy and the National Accounts*. Paris: OECD.

Boeschoten, W.C., and M.M.G. Fase (1984). *The Volume of Payments and the Informal Economy in the Netherlands, 1965–1982*. Dordrecht: Nijhoff.

Cagan, P. (1958). The Demand for Currency Relative to the Total Money Supply. *Journal of Political Economy* 66: 303–29.

Caragata, P.J. (1998a). *Why Are Your Taxes Too High?* Wellington: Seascape Press.

——— (1998b). *The Economic and Compliance Consequences of Taxation: A Report on the Health of the Tax System in New Zealand*. Wellington: Inland Revenue Department.

Caragata, P.J., and D.E.A. Giles (1996). Simulating the Relationship between the Hidden Economy and the Tax Mix in New Zealand. Working Papers on the Health of the Tax System, No. 22. Wellington: Inland Revenue Department.

Chote, R. (1995). Black Economy Believed to Exceed $100bn. *Financial Times* (10–11 June).

Contini, B. (1981). The Second Economy of Italy. *Taxing and Spending* 3: 17–24.

Feige, E.L. (1979). How Big is the Irregular Economy? *Challenge* 22: 5–13.

——— (1982). A New Perspective on Macroeconomic Phenomena: the Theory and Measurement of the Unobserved Economy in the United States: Causes, Consequences and Implications. In M. Walker (ed.), *International Burden of Government* (Vancouver, BC: The Fraser Institute): 112–36.

Frey, B.S., and W.W. Pommerehne (1982). Measuring the Hidden Economy: Though There be Madness, Yet is There Method in it? In V. Tanzi (ed.), *The Underground Economy in the United States and Abroad* (Lexington: Heath): 3–27.

——— (1984). The Hidden Economy: State and Prospects for Measurement. *Review of Income and Wealth* 30: 1–23.

Frey, B.S., and H. Weck-Hannemann (1984). The Hidden Economy as an "Unobserved" Variable. *European Economic Review* 26: 33–53.

Fuà, G. (1976). *Occupazione e Capacità Produttiva: La Realtà Italiana*. Bologna: Il Mulino.

Gaertner, W., and A. Wenig, eds. (1985). *The Economics of the Shadow Economy*. Heidelberg: Springer-Verlag.

Giles, D.E.A.(1997a). The Hidden Economy and the Tax-Gap in New Zealand: A Latent Variable Analysis. Working Paper 97–08. Department of Economics, University of Victoria.

————— (1997b). Causality between the Measured and Underground Economies in New Zealand. *Applied Economics Letters* 4: 63–67.

————— (1997c). Testing for Asymmetry in the Measured and Underground Business Cycles in New Zealand. *Economic Record* 72: 225–32.

————— (1997d). The Hidden Economy and Tax-Evasion Prosecutions in New Zealand. *Applied Economics Letters* 4: 281–85.

————— (1997e). Modelling the Tax Compliance/Non-Compliance Profiles of Audited New Zealand Firms: Evidence from the ORACLE Database. Mimeograph. Department of Economics, University of Victoria.

————— (1998). The Rise and Fall of the New Zealand Underground Economy: Are the Responses Symmetric? Forthcoming in *Applied Economics Letters*.

Giles, D.E.A., and P.J. Caragata (1996). The Learning Path of the Hidden Economy: Tax and Growth Effects in New Zealand. Working Paper No. 21. Wellington: Inland Revenue Department.

Goldberger, A.S. (1972). *Structural Equation Methods in the Social Sciences*. Amsterdam: North-Holland.

Internal Revenue Service (1996). Individual Income Tax Gap Estimates for 1985, 1988 and 1992. Publication 1415 (Rev. 4/96), Doc. 96–13553. Washington, DC: Research Division, Internal Revenue Service.

Isachsen, A.J., J. Kloveland, and S. Strøm (1982). The Hidden Economy in Norway. In V. Tanzi (ed.), *The Underground Economy in the United States and Abroad* (Lexington: Heath): 209–31.

Jöreskog, K., and A.S. Goldberger (1975). Estimation of a Model with Multiple Indicators and Multiple Causes of a Single Latent Variable. *Journal of the American Statistical Association* 70: 631–39.

Jöreskog, K., and D. Sörbom (1993). *LISREL 8: Structural Equation Modeling with the SIMPLIS Command Language*. Chicago: Scientific Software International.

Kirchgaessner, G. (1984). Verfahren zur Erfassung des in der Schattenwirtschaft Erabeiteten Sozial Produkts. *Allgemeines Statistisches Archiv* 68: 378–405.

Lippert, O., and M. Walker, eds. (1997). *The Underground Economy: Global Evidence of its Size and Impact*. Vancouver, BC: The Fraser Institute.

Macafee, K. (1980). A Glimpse of the Hidden Economy in the National Accounts. *Economic Trends* 316: 81–87.

Macecish, G. (1962). Demand for Money and Taxation in Canada. *Southern Economic Journal* 29: 33–38.

Mirus, R., and R.S. Smith (1994). Canada's Underground Economy Revisited: Update and Critique. *Canadian Public Policy* 20: 235–52.

————— (1997). Canada's Underground Economy: Measurement and Implications. In O. Lippert and M. Walker (eds.), *The Underground Economy: Global Evidence of its Size and Impact* (Vancouver, BC: The Fraser Institute): 3–10.

Morgensen, G.V. (1985). *Sort Arbejde i Danmark*. Copenhagen: Nyt Nordisk Forlag.

Park, T. (1979). Reconciliation between Personal Income and Taxable Income, 1947-1977. Mimeograph. Washington, DC: Bureau of Economic Analysis.

Schneider, F. (1997). Empirical Results for the Size of the Shadow Economy of Western European Countries over Time. Discussion Paper 9710. Institut für Volkswirtschaftslehre, Linz University.

Schneider, F., and W.W. Pommerehne (1985). The Decline of Productivity Growth and the Rise of the Shadow Economy in the US. Mimeograph. University of Århus.

Spiro, P.S. (1993). Evidence of a post-GST Increase in the Underground Economy. *Canadian Tax Journal* 41: 247–58.

Tanzi, V. (1980). The Underground Economy in the United States: Estimates and Implications. *Banca Nazionale del Lavoro* 135: 427–53.

——— (1983). The Underground Economy in the United States: Annual Estimates, 1930–1980. *I.M.F. Staff Papers* 30: 283–305.

Tedds, L.M. (1998). Modelling the Canadian Underground Economy. Extended Essay. Department of Economics, University of Victoria.

Weck, H. (1983). *Schattenwirtschaft: Eine Möglichkeit zur Einschränkung der Öffentlichen Verwaltung?* Berne: Peter Lang Verlag.

Zellner, A. (1970). Estimation of Regression Relationships Containing Unobservable Variables. *International Economic Review* 11: 441–54.

Provincial Politicians Describe Recent Fiscal History

Lessons from Alberta on Fiscal Dividends and Taxation

THE HONOURABLE STOCKWELL DAY

In this chapter, I want to pass on some lessons from Alberta about fiscal dividends and taxation. But, let me state my biases right up front. I am a strong believer that small governments are better governments. I do not believe that more money necessarily produces better results. I do not believe that for every problem there is a made-in-government solution.

I believe Canadians—and that includes Albertans—are over-taxed. Particularly when I look at the results governments achieve with tax dollars and when I look at our nearest competition, the United States, I am convinced that governments with too much money will spend it unless they are fenced in by legislation. Further, in Canada today there is no government with extra money: so-called surpluses or fiscal dividends dwindle when compared to the debt burden Canadian governments have left for future generations to pay off, complete with massive interest costs. So, that is where I come from personally. It is a view many Albertans share and that is why they keep electing conservative governments.

Key points in Alberta's recent fiscal history

Early 1980s—the boom times

- Alberta's spending grew with the price of oil and gas.

- We spent as if there was no chance of the economy slowing down.

- People talked about the possibility of oil reaching $80 a barrel.

- Inflation was in the double digits and annual increases to education, health, and other spending areas were in the 10 percent to 15 percent range.

- By 1985/1986, Alberta's spending climbed to over $6,000 per person, among the highest in the country.

- The size of government administration grew to 38,000.

Mid- to late-1980s—"The Bust"

- The price of oil crashed and Alberta's revenues dropped from over $14 billion to $10 billion in less than a year.

- The National Energy Program was another shot at Alberta's economy that devastated the oil and gas sector by not allowing market prices to prevail.

- Government spending was not reduced to make up the shortfall. Instead, we counted on optimistic revenue forecasts and thought the downturn would be short lived.

- Nine years of deficits resulted in a total of $19.5 billion in borrowing.

- Increasing taxes in 1987 to fight the deficit was a failure.

1993—reality hits

- Alberta reports a deficit of $3.4 billion and net debt of $8.7 billion, with an accumulated debt (1986–1993) of $19.5 billion.

- Debt servicing costs on the $19.5 billion we borrowed had skyrocketed from $40 million to $1.5 billion in only 9 years.

- Costly overlap and duplication were evident across all sectors of the public service from schools to hospitals to colleges and within government itself.

- Government was everywhere, in every aspect of the lives of Albertans. We were involved in things we never should have: selling alcohol, providing business loans and guarantees, tinkering with the economy, running businesses such as registries to sell drivers' licenses or land titles.

- Government had lost credibility and the trust of its electors because it could not balance the books. We thought the way out was to promise more, but what Albertans really wanted was for us to get rid of the deficit, not pass on a staggering debt burden to our children, and deliver affordable services.

The 1990s—balanced budgets and fiscal responsibility

Alberta's balanced budget plan focused on:

- cutting spending by 20 percent while setting clear priorities: fewer cuts in core areas like health and education and more in areas that were not essential;

- reducing waste and duplication and getting out of businesses others could do better;

- using conservative revenue forecasts and building-in cushions on corporate income tax and non-renewable resource revenue so we would not see a repeat of 1986/87;

- paying down debt.

What are the results?

- We have gone from being among the highest spending province in Canada to one of the lower spending and from the biggest government in Canada to the smallest.

- The deficit was eliminated ahead of schedule, thanks to a combination of spending cuts, a strong oil and gas sector, and a more balanced and diversified economy

- Taxes were not increased and Alberta still prides itself on having the lowest taxes in Canada across the board and no sales tax.

- By March of 1999, we shall have paid off $8.7 million on our net debt though we shall still have $13 billion more in asset-supported debt to repay.

- Alberta's economy is booming—and that means the good news of annual surpluses.

- The size of government administration has decreased by 14,000 positions to 24,000.

- Three-year business plans, budgets, and annual reports on performance and results have become standard features of the budget process.

- We have reduced costly duplication and inefficiencies and moved out of businesses we never should have been in.

• Reinvestment has begun. Albertans are starting to see the direct benefits of paying down debt. Interest savings go to priorities like health and education. Last year that meant 1000 more front-line workers in the health system and better access to surgeries and other treatments.

Five lessons from Alberta

(1) There's no right time to cut government spending.

In tough economic times, there's pressure on governments to "do something"—stimulate the economy, create jobs, build infrastructure, "give people a leg up." In good times, there is money available so there is no urgent need to reduce spending. An article in *The Economist* says: "The state grows in bad times, it seems, because it has to. It grows in good times as well, only faster, because governments feel more ambitious." (September 20, 1997: 11)

In Alberta, the financial crisis was the best reason to do what we should have been doing all along—spending only what we could afford and protecting the taxpayers' hard-earned dollars. The financial crisis gave us a good reason to say "no" even to very good ideas. And, it forced us to go back to the drawing board and ask the tough questions about results and about the role government should play.

(2) Understand what your business is—and is not.

In the past 50 years, governments around the world have grown and expanded—have become more and more involved in the lives of its citizens. In Alberta, we took over alcohol sales, selling drivers' licenses and trying to "control the economy." It did not work. We learned that you cannot do all the same things you have always done and spend less money. We learned others—individuals, families, municipalities, organizations, volunteer groups, and the private sector—can often do the job better than government.

(3) Focus on results.

This is a big step for governments to take because it means challenging the conventional wisdom that says spend more and you will get better quality programs and better results. That is the kind of thinking Bill Thorsell talked about in one of his editorials: "When money becomes the measure of all things, we dumbly equate more money spent to superior quality and virtue" (*Globe and Mail*, September 13, 1997: D6). He makes the analogy to computers and electronic equipment. No one assumes that a personal computer is inferior because it costs one-half of what it did five years ago. In fact, we expect it to offer more features and more power at half the price. The same is true for other retail products. But, when it comes to goods and services in the public sector, we blindly reject the view that lower cost can mean better value.

In Alberta, we are working hard to shift the focus from how much we spend to the results we achieve. This means introducing a more business-like approach to business plans and budgets. We set a three-year horizon and an overall business plan and budget for government; we require every ministry to develop a concise business plan setting out the results that they expect to achieve and the strategies that they will use. And, we report on performance and results every year, publishing one overall report for government and a separate report for every ministry. Measures are tracked so we can see where we are achieving the results we planned and where we are failing short. These results are made public for all Albertans to see.

Alberta's Auditor General audits our measurements and goals and we produce an annual report, *Measuring Up*, that is released along with our year-end audited financial statements.

(4) Build strong fences

This lesson is important not so much for the people outside the fence but for those on the inside—the politicians. It is not easy sticking to a conservative, no-frills budget. Most politicians are tempted to spend more and there is no shortage of good ways to spend money in our families, our businesses, or our governments. Alberta's strong fences are legislation that forbids us to run a deficit, requires us to report on finances every quarter, requires conservative revenue forecasts, requires annual debt payments, and sets out clear accountability requirements.

(5) Once you have cut, do not think the job is done.

Right now in Alberta, the word "surplus" is a Provincial Treasurer's nightmare. People quickly forget the tough times we have been through and, with more money available, they want us to spend more. There is no permanent fix, therefore, because the temptation to spend has not gone away and the expectations of some people, some organizations or sectors, or even some MLAs are always present.

A case for smaller governments

Let me close by going back to the key points I made at the beginning. I am not a supporter of big governments. I think we are over-taxed as Canadians. And I am convinced we can achieve as good or better results while spending less money.

Why is it that Canadians resist tax reductions?

Canadians want the debt reduced but they fear a loss of services. They do not see the complete "loop" from less tax to a more vibrant economy to more dollars available for social infrastructure.

Some may have read the article, The Future of the State, in *The Economist* (September 20, 1997). If you have not, I highly recommend it because it looks at the steady growth in government and asks some critical questions about why this has happened and what results it has had. Some of the key points from that article are points we all need to think about if we are trying to answer the question: What is the optimal size of government?

- Government spending has moved ever upward, no matter what the conditions: during war and peace, with free trade and little trade, in big countries and small, government spending went up everywhere.

- Even Margaret Thatcher was not able to stem the tide. After 20 years of cuts in Britain, government spending as a proportion of the total economy dropped by only 1 percent.

- In Canada, government spending as a percentage of GDP has grown from 13 percent in 1920 to almost 45 percent in 1996.

- Governments that are spending heavily seem to be doing little or no better than governments that spend much less in providing social goods—better education or better health care. And, there is no evidence that the people governments are often trying to help—the poor—are any better off.

The Economist's conclusion is that

> [i]n the West, it seems, original sin has been superseded; instead, people come into the world with an original burden of obligation to the social enterprise, a debt to their fellow citizens that is not of their own making and that they can never discharge. Though not without its comforts, it is a kind of bondage. It augers well for big government. (The Future of the State, *The Economist*: 48)

I am not as pessimistic as *The Economist*. I am convinced we can eliminate or at least reduce the "original burden." I believe we owe it to our children to do so.

Five steps for escaping debt

(1) Reduce taxes. Governments cannot spend what they do not have.

(2) Set clear expectations. It is time to re-think the role of government—a role that should be smaller not greater than it is now.

(3) Establish a clear program of tough outcome measurements.

(4) Erect a legislative fence to put strength into policy statements like deficit elimination, budget procedures, debt pay-down, and taxpayer protection

(5) Resist temptation. It is always easier to say "yes" than it is to say "no." Politicians are no different from anyone else but it is our job to provide leadership, to resist the easy way out, and to stick to the hard-fought gains each of us has made in each of our provinces over the past four or five years.

The hard work is just beginning.

Balance: Fiscal Responsibility in Saskatchewan

The Honourable Janice MacKinnon

The 1990s have seen an encouraging trend by Canadian governments towards fiscal responsibility though we have used different approaches to accomplish this. Now we face the new challenge of ensuring that our economies continue to grow and to provide Canadians with economic opportunities not only today but also through the next century. In Saskatchewan, we are taking on that challenge in much the same way that we managed our fiscal situation. In this chapter, I shall first describe where we were and what we did. Then, I want to describe how we are taking the same kind of approach—one of balance—to growing the economy.

At the end of 1991, when the Saskatchewan New Democratic Party took office, our province faced three major challenges:

- the largest per-capita deficit in Canada
- the largest per-capita debt in Canada
- business had stopped investing and creating jobs.

This called for difficult choices. The top priority was to stop the financial bleeding. We also wanted to take a balanced approach and to protect the most vulnerable of our citizens. We could not balance the books on the backs of the sick, the aged, young people, and the unemployed. To achieve this balance, we had to be innovative. Together with the Saskatchewan people, communities, businesses, and co-operatives, we designed a four-year, balanced plan to restore our finances.

In some cases, we reduced expenditures; in others, we redesigned programs; in still other cases, we increased revenues. We cut spending dramatically. We redesigned our health system but our decision was to protect our vital social-safety net. Overall, not one dollar was cut from the social envelope from the time we took office.

The choices were difficult but we believed that it was essential to set the stage for growth by putting our financial house in order. We were the first senior government in Canada to balance our budget and the first to start paying down debt.

When our finances stabilized, business started to invest once more and our economy started to grow. By 1996, Saskatchewan led all provinces with 3.3 percent growth in GDP, more than double the national average. Manufacturing shipments were up 10 percent, the highest increase in Canada. This trend continued in 1997. Manufacturing shipments are running 18 percent higher than the same period last year, an increase well above the national average of 7 percent. Retail sales are also up almost ten percent year over year.

Our credit rating has, once again, been upgraded. When Standard and Poor's raised our rating this year, they cited the sharp decline in tax supported debt and our commitment to debt reduction as part of the reason. So with our fiscal house in order, it is time to shift our focus more clearly to the economy, taking the same balanced approach that we used in managing our fiscal situation.

Our balanced approach reflects our view that the role of government goes beyond "just getting out of the way" or "counting the dollars." But, at the same time, government cannot be all things to all people, an approach that leads along the dangerous road of mounting debt or mounting tax loads.

We will continue to produce balanced budgets—that is essential. But, our budget surpluses are being divided into roughly equal thirds:

- one-third to debt reduction

- one-third to reducing taxes

- one third to investing in people

It is our view that, without this balanced approach, you cannot really grow the economy. As governments, one of our responsibilities is to ensure that we are competitive.

A recent study by the KPMG company analyzed the costs of doing business in Saskatchewan, compared to competing centres in Canada and the United States.

For all 10 economic sectors examined, Saskatchewan's cities offer lower operating costs than competing cities in the United States. In fact, costs were 12 percent lower in Saskatchewan than in the United States, in part because in Saskatchewan the government pays the costs of health care while in the United States, the private sector pays for health-care premiums. Saskatchewan was also competitive with other Canadian jurisdictions. For instance, the cost of starting a business in Saskatchewan is 18 percent less than in Winnipeg and 29 percent less than in Calgary.

There are a number of factors that go into the mix on competitiveness. A major factor, however, is taxation. We have made a commitment to affordable tax reduction and we have acted on that commitment. We have used targeted tax reductions in key sectors of our economy such as manufacturing and processing and call centres so that, in these sectors, Saskatchewan is one of the least expensive jurisdictions in North America in which to do business.

We have also committed ourselves to making more broadly based tax reductions when they are affordable. In 1995 and 1996, we made modest income tax cuts. In 1997, we cut our provincial sales tax from 9 to 7 percent—a decrease of 22 percent—and it is now the second lowest in Canada. And we have seen growth in consumer confidence as a result.

Clearly, tax reduction is important but it must not be made at the expense of debt reduction. Paying down the debt is really an investment in the future since it provides the long-term fiscal stability that is so critical to long-term growth. Government's role is to preserve this.

And as we head into the new century, government must also invest strategically. By "strategically" I mean that, because government cannot be all things to all people, we must invest in areas like education and training that show the most promise for future opportunities. Across the country, we are facing the double-barreled challenge of a lack of trained workers in some sectors and continued high unemployment in others and we need continually to improve, to modify and to invest in education and training.

Saskatchewan has a training strategy in place that is designed to provide training that is more relevant to industry needs. It is not perfect but we are improving it through partnerships between business and our academic institutions. The skills need to match the jobs if we are going to grow; one of the first things that growth-oriented companies look at is the availability of skilled people.

A growing economy also requires solid infrastructure. In Canada generally and especially in Saskatchewan, where we rely so heavily upon trade, transportation is vital. We are investing $2.5 billion in our highways over the 10 ten years. We have also asked the federal government to develop a national transportation strategy; Canada is the only federal state in the western world in which there is no national highways program.

Sixty percent of Saskatchewan's gross domestic product is sold outside the province; sixty percent of that goes to international markets. One out of every 3 jobs in Saskatchewan depends upon trade. For this reason, in partnership with industry, we established the Saskatchewan Trade and Export Partnership, Canada's first partnership between industry and government to promote trade. Finding and expanding markets is critical to our growth in the next century.

Innovation is also important as it is essential to capturing and keeping markets. It is the key to becoming or remaining competitive and so, in today's competitive economy, government must build and sustain the capacity to innovate. Saskatchewan has made a significant investment in research and development, especially in areas like agricultural biotechnology.

We are now seeing what we think is just the tip of the iceberg when it comes to the return on this kind of investment. One-third of Canada's agricultural biotechnology industry is now located in Saskatchewan; we have attracted major global players to invest and locate in Saskatchewan. We created the world's first genetically engineered crop; the world's first genetically engineered animal vaccines. We are using the tools and products of innovation to help feed a hungry world; we are creating new and better crops for more productive farming, new and better uses for those crops to diversify our economy.

Just how far we have come is demonstrated in the selection of the University of Saskatchewan by an international peer review panel to be the site of Canada's only synchrotron, a sophisticated x-ray light source that can examine sub-atomic structures. It will give us the ability, for example, to produce frost-resistant crops more quickly and to speed up our search for cancer-fighting drugs. Its potential benefits to the biotechnology sector are enormous.

Strategic investment has certainly been the key to success in agricultural biotechnology and research and development. We take this same strategic approach in managing our finances and in our role in the economy overall.

So when you ask how we should we spend the fiscal dividend, our answer is that we should invest strategically to create the conditions for economic growth in the twenty-first century.

Economic growth is more than an end in itself. It is through economic growth that we can offer services that help create a high quality of life while keeping taxes at a reasonable level. In turn, those same services help us to grow, as our subsidized health-care costs make us more competitive than many American locations.

Balance is essential. Too great a focus on any one area creates distortion and over time the economy suffers, and society suffers. Maintaining the balance is a challenge for governments. But our future depends upon it, both as a province and as a nation. We already have a strong foundation. Canada has been ranked as the best place in the world to live. With the right approach, we can achieve a vibrant economy in which there are opportunities for all.

Restructuring the Government in Ontario

THE HONOURABLE ERNIE EVES

There has been a great deal of discussion of late about how the federal government should spend its expected fiscal dividend. Paul Martin, the Finance Minister, is getting advice from every side and appears to be thinking about a combination of debt reduction, tax cuts, and spending.

I am pleased to join in the discussion. Unfortunately, unlike my colleagues from Saskatchewan and Alberta, I am not in a position to write about what we have been doing with our fiscal dividend. Ontario got off to a late start in this endeavour.

Undoubtedly, the early 1990s was a period of economic turbulence for all of North America but several factors deepened the impact on Ontario and a series of poor provincial policy decisions exacerbated our problems. Ontario remained largely oblivious as the world changed between 1985 and 1995, as global trends took hold—trends of great significance to the people of Ontario—and as many provinces like Alberta and Saskatchewan and numerous members of the Organisation for Economic Cooperation and Development (OECD) changed the way they operated in response to these competitive pressures.

The Progressive Conservative government came to power in Ontario in June of 1995, the year after Saskatchewan and Alberta balanced their budgets. Both of those provinces were then beginning to see the benefits of their hard work. In the fiscal year 1994/1995, Alberta had a surplus equal to 1.2 percent of GDP and Saskatchewan had a surplus of 0.6 percent of GDP.

What did Ontario have? Increasing deficits and debt. Between 1990 and 1995 our ration of debt to GDP doubled and, in 1995, Ontario had a deficit of 3.4 percent of GDP. Ontario was spending nearly one-fifth of its revenues on interest payments alone. The deficit was over 11 billion dollars and the provincial debt was 100 billion dollars. The deficit was so large that we were spending over a million dollars an hour more than we were taking in revenues.

Residents of Ontario also paid some of the highest taxes in North America. Between 1985 and 1995, taxes overall were raised a 65 times in Ontario. Between 1988 and 1993, Ontario's basic tax rate rose 7 percentage points while it rose an average of only 2 percentage points for all of the other provinces.

There was one thing we did not have in Ontario—jobs. Despite our central location in the North American market, our diversified economy, our strong infrastructure, and our skilled workforce, Ontario's economic performance between 1990 and 1994 was the worst since the Great Depression. In fact, the number of people working in the province at the end of 1994 was lower than it was at the beginning of 1990. Between 1990 and 1995, employment in the private sector fell by 38,000.

Clearly we faced serious problems and we had difficult choices to make. It was obvious that the only way to unleash the forces of private sector for growth, to make Ontario a competitive jurisdiction in the global economy, and to maintain the high level of social services offered here, was through a profound restructuring of the way that government operated. With this in view, as it prepared for the 1995 provincial election, the Progressive Conservative party embarked upon the development of an platform of government restructuring. We asked whether there were more efficient ways to deliver the important programs to Ontario. Were there fairer ways to approach taxation? Were there changes in social infrastructure that would reduce waste and enhance outcomes? Most important of all, we asked whether it was possible to balance the unique social and economic interests of our province while creating jobs and balancing the budget?

We looked to a number of jurisdictions in order to develop our recovery plan. We looked at hospital restructuring in places like Saskatchewan, the business planning process implemented in Alberta and issues like labour policy in other Canadian provinces. We studied what worked and what did not in New Zealand, in Europe, and in Asia. We looked at public policy in places like New Jersey.

The plan that we developed was a combination of ideas used in other places and adapted to the specific needs of Ontarians. Our plan was one that many thought was impossible to implement: to cut taxes, to reduce spending, and to restructure government—all at the same time.

In our first two and one-half years, we cut government spending drastically and are dramatically reducing its size. We have already cut taxes a total of 30 times in just two Budgets. We are completely restructuring our relationship with local governments and delineating responsibility for services best provided at the municipal level. We have refocused funding for social assistance, implemented a process of business planning for every government ministry, rebalanced labour laws, and taken steps to eliminate over 1500 unnecessary regulations.

The results have been remarkable: in the midst of the largest government restructuring ever undertaken, consumer confidence has risen for 7 consecutive quarters to its highest level in nearly 9 years, up 37 percent since the end of 1995. Ontario's real GDP rose at an annual rate of 7.2 percent in the second quarter of 1997, following growth of 6.8 percent in the first quarter. The total number of people working in Ontario has risen two percent in the past year in spite of major, ongoing, reduction in the number of jobs in the public sector. Since implementing the first phase of our cuts in the income-tax rate, revenues from all forms of taxation have increased by over $1.2 billion.

The consensus of economic forecasts expects Ontario to grow at 4.4 percent in 1998, compared to 3.7 percent for Canada. For the period from 1997 to 2001, the consensus predicts average growth of 3.7 percent in Ontario, compared to 2.5 percent for the United States and an average of 2.3 percent for the rest of the G7 countries.

We have now proven that governments can cut taxes and spending at the same time, and still see an increase in revenue as the private sector creates more and better jobs. In Ontario, tax cuts are building confidence and economic momentum to boost private-sector growth as we reduce spending. Lower tax rates provide increased incentives for investment, entrepreneurship, and innovation. These lead in turn to a more dynamic economy and a permanently higher growth rate rather than to short-term job creation.

We have recently received credit from federal Industry Minister John Manley for having had this insight—and having acted on it. Mr. Manley was recently quoted as giving the Ontario government credit for Ontario's leading the nation during 1998 with what the Bank of Montreal called "red hot" commercial growth. Mr. Manley is quoted as saying Ontario taxpayers "have more money in their pockets and therefore they have more money to spend." He went on to confirm that in his view "tax cuts increase domestic consumption."

Ontario's advice to the federal government, then, is quite simple: cut taxes. In our view, one of the first federal tax cuts should be to Employment Insurance premiums. Employment Insurance premiums are payroll taxes, period. There is room for a reduction much larger than the last two cuts the federal government has announced. Along with the Canadian Federation of Independent Business and other business organizations, we have argued for a premium reduction to $2.20 per $100 of insurable earnings, much lower than the $2.70 announced last month to take effect in January. There is also ample room for the federal government to eliminate entirely the Employment Insurance premiums for youths, creating jobs for young Canadians now. Even were both these cuts made, the federal government would continue to run a surplus in the EI account.

The federal government does not have to have a fiscal dividend to cut taxes. We believe they are in a position to cut payroll taxes now, especially when they are increasing Canada Pension Plan premiums. While Mr Martin has indicated that the huge Employment Insurance surplus is an important part of the government's fiscal plan, certainly with a budget surplus there will be no reason not to cut taxes.

Spend the fiscal dividend?

Let me turn for a moment to the reported spending plans for the federal fiscal dividend. I must admit that I become concerned when I hear that the federal government is considering new spending. If we have learned a lesson from the 1980s, it is that we must not squander the revenues that good times bring. Ontario's experience has proven that governments often find ways to spend money even if they do not have it.

Having said that, when the federal government is looking to spend, Ontario would offer the following advice. Be strategic. Do not just layer new programs on top of the old without testing whether the old programs remain useful, effective, and efficient. In Ontario and Alberta, the governments have implemented a rigorous business planning process for each ministry. This process identifies objectives and targets to measure results. It ensures accountability and identifies programs that are no longer relevant to the needs of citizens.

Government provides a vital role in a well-ordered society. However, there is little doubt that in recent decades we have had too much government. The benefits from specific government programs are concentrated while the taxpaying burden is spread out. In spite of that, in recent years the general dismay of taxpayers about excessive spending and debt has become influential. This is a sign that governments have grown much larger than they ought to be.

Two researchers at the International Monetary Fund have published a fascinating historical study of the growth of governments in the leading industrialized countries over the past century. Based on their studies, they arrived at the tentative conclusion that "the level of public spending does not need to be much higher than, say, 30 percent of GDP to achieve most of the important social and economic objectives that justify governmental intervention."

Needless to say, spending by government in Canada remains far above 30 percent. In Ontario alone, it represents 16 percent of GDP (down from 18.6 percent in 1995). The study goes on to predict that the radical reforms needed to bring government down to this level will generate "strong opposition, from the specific groups that benefit from the spending ... The argument that the reforms would make most citizens better off over the long run will not allay concerns in the short run." In Ontario, we are very familiar with this opposition but we will press on to do what is best for the economy and for the citizens of Ontario.

Debt reduction

The government in Ontario is looking forward to the day when we can begin to pay down our debt. Ontario's ratio of debt to GDP was stable between 15 and 17 percent for two decades before the 1990s. Then, from 1990, it doubled in five years. Our debt now stands at over 31 percent of GDP. This makes us vulnerable in the event of future economic shocks, and it means that an unacceptably high share of our spending goes to paying interest.

The federal government's debt to GDP ratio is actually more than double ours—70 percent. For obvious reasons then, the federal government must take a serious approach to debt reduction once the deficit is eliminated.

On the question of how far governments should go in the eliminating debt, some may argue that it is in not advisable for governments to completely eliminate their debts. They would argue that it is appropriate and advisable that government—like business—continue to carry some debt. Moreover, governments invest in infrastructure that lasts for many years. It makes sense to pay for this type of investment by borrowing and spreading the cost over the useful life of the investment.

In Ontario, we are committed to bringing our debt ratio back down to its historical norm in a reasonable number of years. In the short term however we are focussing on getting rid of entirely our deficit by the year 2000/2001. We have already cut more than 40 percent or $4.7 billion below the $11.3 billion deficit the government was faced with when we took office. The 1997 Budget projected a $6.6 billion deficit for this year. Our first quarter results have indicated that we are on track and our second quarter results will show that, in fact, we are ahead of our target.

While we are not in the enviable surplus position of the federal government, Alberta, Saskatchewan and many other provinces, we are on track to meet our balanced budget goal. We are eliminating the deficit in a manageable fashion and reducing the size of government.

To date we have cut our own administrative spending by 33 percent and have reduced our own bureaucracy by more than 17 percent or 14,000 full time positions. At the same time we are making significant reinvestment in priority services and restructuring that will save us money in the future and provide us with important returns today.

For example we are investing well over $2 billion into health care, and an additional $140 million this year for essential services like dialysis, transplants, and cardiac services. Over four years we are investing over two and a half billion in municipal restructuring.

In our last two budgets we announced major re-investments in education including $650 million for school capital, $300 million for the Ontario Student Opportunities Trust Fund and $500 million for the provincial share of the Research and Development Challenge Fund.

At the same time we are cutting taxes in a variety of areas. We are not only cutting personal income tax rates, we are cutting payroll taxes —including the Employer Health Tax on the first $400,000 of payroll— and we are implementing sectoral tax cuts.

In the R& D and high tech sectors for example, I announced no less than seven tax cuts in the 1997 Budget including the Capital Tax Deduction for Research and Development, the Computer Animation and Special Effects Tax Credit, the Ontario new Technology tax incentive and the Ontario Business Research Institute Tax Credit.

These tax cuts will make Ontario one of the most R&D friendly jurisdictions in the entire world. We are implementing the Ontario Film Tax Credit to ensure that we maintain our position as one of the leading film and television production locations in North America.

In doing all of this at the same time we have proven that a balanced budget need not be achieved at the expense of jobs and growth.

So let me sum up by saying that Ontario believes the best approach to investing our national fiscal dividend should be a balanced one.

- Cut taxes to create jobs—it works.
- Be very cautious and focus on accountability when considering options for spending.
- Set a debt target and work towards it in a manageable fashion.

Finally I would say that the most important thing for all jurisdictions to remember, regardless of their fiscal position is that, in fact, government has no money. It only has the money it takes from the people. That money belongs to the people and more often than not is best left for them to decide what to do with it.

Discussion of Lessons from Provincial Politicians

Editor's Note: The following draws on a transcript of a round-table discussion that took place after the luncheon address by the Hon. Ernie Eves. I have edited all questions and answers heavily to make them brief and concise and I apologize for the omission of much wit, repartee, and rhetoric that brightened the live proceedings. The politicians have given their approval of the edited version of their remarks.

Question 1

Michael Walker   As was pointed out this morning, a very significant fraction of the total adjustment in the federal Government's fiscal position was effectively accomplished through cuts in its transfers to the other levels of government. These cuts pushed the adjustment problem down to a lower level. What is the Ministers' response to this policy?

Response

Hon. Stockwell Day   The federal Government made drastic cuts in Canadian health and social transfers—amounting to about 35 percent. In other areas of federal program spending, reductions were somewhere between 5 percent and 7 percent. In Alberta we criticized this distribution of cuts and the failure to reduce some types of what Canadians considered to be unnecessary programs.

Hon. Janice MacKinnon   Our concern in Saskatchewan was very similar. As I recall, about 14 percent of the federal budget is spent on health, education, and social programming and yet in the last two budgets more than three-quarters of cuts were in that 14 percent of spending that affects provinces. It is surprising that the federal government got away with these cuts since they involve health, education, and social programs, which Canadians care about very much.

We persuaded the people in our own province on this point but I do not think we succeeded nationally: many Canadians seem unable to relate the problems in health care that occur at the provincial level to the real authors of the problem, the federal government.

Hon. Ernie Eves   It will sound like a broken record and we are not here to bash the federal Government, but there is no doubt that the federal Government has not done nearly the job that the provinces have done in cutting their own administrative expenditure. Between the fiscal years 1994/95 and 1997/98, the federal Government will have reduced Canadian health and social transfers to provinces by over 37 percent. During the same period, they have reduced their own administrative spending 3 percent. Compare that with the Ontario government, which reduced its administrative spending by 33 percent.

I believe that as a matter of policy and principle the federal Government should have looked first in its own backyard to reduce spending. The governments of the province of Ontario, whether it was under Bob Rae or Mike Harris, have not really complained very much about these cuts. We had to deal with reality as we found it. We know that the federal Government will not return transfers to their previous levels so we will have to deal with this reality. I do not think that the federal Government policies are fair and equitable nor do I think the distribution of cuts makes good economic sense.

Currently the annualized surplus in Employment Insurance Premiums is $5 billion to $7 billion. When he was a member of the opposition, Paul Martin said that payroll taxes like EI premiums are job killers. His own ministry officials indicate that if these taxes were reduced to traditional levels it would create 200,000 to 300,000 jobs nationally. Such a policy would create economic benefits for everyone, including the federal Government.

Question 2

Grant Hill, MP   The Krever Commission Report was just published. The federal Government as well as provincial governments took some blame for the blood transfusion tragedy. Allan Rock, the federal Minister of Health, says that before compensation can be paid to the victims of the tragedy he will have to consult with the provinces. It is interesting that yesterday Quebec passed a unanimous motion in their National Assembly saying that they will pay compensation to their affected citizens. As the Reform critic for health-care policies, I wonder how the governments of the three provinces that you represent here are likely to deal with the problem of compensation for the victims of Hepatitis C?

Response

Hon. Ernie Eves The province of Ontario will do ultimately what is right and responsible but I also think it is a shared problem and I will be interested to hear the federal Government's definition of shared responsibility. If it is as it was in social transfers, I will not be too impressed. I look forward to seeing their proposal along these lines. Obviously the Minister of Health will bring it to the Cabinet for consideration.

Hon. Stockwell Day We have not had a recommendation yet from our Health Minister. However, the question raises the important and much broader issue of liability of governments for past events. In Alberta we have a number of such events and they involve potentially a large hidden deficit that we have not even begun to deal with. Decisions have to be reached on how far back in history such events can be made to impose liabilities on current generations of taxpayers.

Question 3

Audience I would like to talk briefly about the Canada Pension Plan because that is something that is a joint federal and provincial responsibility. Once the system begins to accumulate a financial surplus, how is it going to be invested? Should it go to provinces as low-interest loans or should it be invested at private-market interest rates? From what I have heard, the Atlantic provinces are lobbying for low-interest loans to them. How do the provincial ministers present here feel about this issue and especially the issue of preventing hidden subsidies through low interest rates going to certain provinces?

Response

Hon. Janice MacKinnon One of the changes to the CPP brought in by the recent federal legislation addressed exactly this issue and stopped loans to provinces at preferred rates. I hope that future finance ministers will ensure the continuation of this policy.

Question 4

Ludger Schuknecht Coming from continental Europe, I must say that I am very impressed with the fiscal consolidation and reform efforts by the federal and provincial governments of Canada. As you know, some countries and regions have introduced fiscal rules, balanced budget rules, or deficit limits to lock in the gains from such consolidation and to avoid temptations that could throw us off-track in the future. Do any of the provinces now have, or plan to have, such rules imposed through legislation?

Response

Hon. Stockwell Day   In Alberta, we have put in place such legislation. It provides for the elimination of the deficit, down-payment of the debt, protection against new taxes, and it even directs the process of making budgets. I have shared with Paul Martin what the merit of such legislation has been. It has provided us with effective means to resist pressures for increased spending and bigger government, which is inevitable when the economy turns up and fiscal surpluses develop.

As Ernie Eves and Janice MacKinnon know, every day there are pressures for more spending. It can become wearying and there is a temptation to want to turn into Santa Claus and start handing out gifts. I am glad that those legislative protections are there. They allow me to smile, hold hands and weep with the groups asking for more money and say: "I'd love to help you but you don't want me in jail." Paul Martin suggested at the federal level that he is not willing to embrace that type of legislated restraint. Personally, I think it is the way to go and our experience in Alberta proves it.

Hon. Janice MacKinnon   In Saskatchewan, we passed legislation that requires us to balance the budget over a four-year cycle. We did this to prevent a recurrence of the developments of the 1980s that got us into fiscal trouble. During that period the Conservative government moved certain expenditures off budget and they used for ordinary expenditures, revenues from the sale of some Crown Corporations. So our legislation specifically prohibits changes to accounting practices and requires that revenues from the sale of assets be applied to debt reduction.

Hon. Stockwell Day   Alberta has adopted measures similar to those used in Saskatchewan. Presently we are drafting legislation that would apply the same principles to other levels of government in the province.

Hon. Ernie Eves   In Ontario, our first priority was the elimination of the deficit. We have exceeded every target we have set for this task. But I can foresee the time coming when we will have to address the issue and introduce balanced budget legislation as well.

Comments

Michael Walker   The Fraser Institute's monthly publication, *Fraser Forum*, the December 1987 edition, has a survey of existing budget-restraint measures and legislative limits on deficits in Canada.

Herb Grubel   I fully support all efforts to erect institutional barriers against deficit spending and accounting changes to hide it. As an MP in the last federal parliament, I introduced a Private Members Bill that would have imposed such restraints on the federal Government. The bill was debated for 20 minutes at the end of a day when the House was empty except for one member from each party. Thereafter the bill died. It did not have the support of the Minister of Finance or his staff.

Question 5

Audience   When are the three finance ministers present here going to address seriously the issue of free interprovincial trade, specifically in the area of government procurement? We can trade a lot easier with the United States than we can among ourselves in Canada. My second question is, when are we going to create a National Securities Commission for Canada? We are the only country in the G7 that does not have such a Commission.

Response

Stockwell Day   On the issue of a National Securities Commission, Alberta has worked closely with Ontario and British Columbia on the design of a protocol to enhance the efficiency of the Canadian capital market. However, we remain concerned that such a Commission not be driven by the interests of central Canada at the expense of Alberta with its special conditions and unique needs for exploration capital.

The issue of interprovincial trade is a source of real frustration. Here is an example. Presently regulators from British Columbia come to Alberta to examine the books of Alberta firms with businesses operations in British Columbia. These BC regulators force the Alberta firms to open their books so that they can establish their adherence to BC minimum wage and other labour market rules. They take special issue with bonus-based compensation rates used widely by Alberta firms with the full support of their employees. These types of activities by regulators from one province invading another are untenable. We have to work to eliminate them.

Hon. Janice MacKinnon   To answer the important question about the optimum level of government, let me note that all politicians have a boss. It is the electorate. We can lead, but we cannot drive it. The people have their own views about a reasonable level of taxation and government services. They prize very highly their quality of life and politicians who do not meet their wishes are not around very long.

Ernie Eves   Returning to the question about the National Securities Commission, I think that the government of Ontario probably is the villain who Stockwell thinks is out to get the people of Alberta. In fact, we have had discussions with the federal Government about a National Securities Commission for as long as I have been the Minister of Finance, or about 2 years. I supported the idea of a National Securities Commission from the beginning. However, there are certain regions of the country that are a little—I do not want to use the word "paranoid" so let me say concerned—about their particular needs for investment. I do not blame them for taking this position but I think that it could be accommodated within the bounds of a National Securities Commission.

We have made some progress towards agreements that will see all provinces work together under a common set of rules and guidelines. In the meantime, there has been a dramatic reform of the Ontario Securities Commission. This reform was undertaken because—quite frankly—we could not afford to wait any longer for the emergence of a consensus on the creation of a National Securities Commission. I hope that such a Commission can still be created because it would be in the long term in best interests of Canadians, regardless of where they live in the country. We need rules to attract and keep capital in Canada.

Question 6

Audience   I have heard the speeches of the Ministers. But sometimes important points are made more effectively if they are spoken off the cuff. So, could I ask the Ministers to summarize briefly their recommendations to the federal Government on how it should spend the so-called fiscal dividend?

Response

Hon. Ernie Eves   "Read Fraser Institute publications more carefully" would be my advice to the federal Government. That is the plug Michael asked me to put in.

I think that the federal Government should pay more attention to the measurable successes that provinces have had in areas of fiscal restraint. These successes contain lessons about workable solutions. They can be applied federally as well as provincially.

Hon. Janice MacKinnon   My recommendations are: be balanced, continue to pay down debt, continue to reduce taxes, but also be prepared to invest strategically in the economy and in the quality of life, and you will be around for a long time.

Question 7

Audience   Could the Ministers please comment on the problems raised by the pending Kyoto Agreements on global climate change, which are likely to have important effects on their provinces?

Response

Hon. Stockwell Day   I do not mind commenting on the issues from Alberta's perspective. Obviously the implications of the agreements for us are huge. The recent move of the federal Government is procedurally absolutely unacceptable: last week the federal government adopted new policies in total disregard of the agreements that had been reached at the federal/provincial meetings in Regina. The government of Alberta was not even informed about the new policies. This treatment has the potential of becoming a national unity issue.

The science of global warming is, at best, suspect, as was discussed in a recent Fraser Institute publication. There is also the issue of the importance of Canada in a global setting: if Canada disappeared under the water of the melting ice-caps tomorrow, global emissions of green house gases would be reduced less than two percent. The benefits from further reductions in Canada's emissions are not very important globally but they would bring serious economic problems for the province of Alberta. At the same time, let me remind you that there already has been considerable voluntary compliance by industry to government norms and this has resulted in major reductions in emissions. Alberta industry is leading in this respect and yet we will be asked to do even more. Other jurisdictions will get exemptions and Alberta industries will move there to escape already existing Alberta regulations. We are very, very concerned about these issues.

Hon. Janice MacKinnon   The federal government's unilateral actions raise question about the viability of the federal/provincial partnership. Time limitations prevent me from going into the substance of the complicated question. Let me just note that the Saskatchewan position differs somewhat from that of Alberta. On this matter we think also that balance is important.

Hon. Ernie Eves   My personal opinion is that Alberta's point of view is not too far from reality. I think that we want to be very sure of scientific evidence on global warming before we set unreasonable standards and spend zillions of dollars to meet some artificial targets. I think we are moving perhaps a little too quickly on this issue. I am not saying we should turn a blind eye to it but that we better proceed in a very cautious and prudent manner.

Views of Business Economists

Options on the Fiscal Dividend

JOHN MCCALLUM

Let me begin by saying what I think the federal Government will do. I think that it will target a never-ending string of balanced budgets. It will do so with extremely prudent assumptions and a sizable contingency reserve, so that if the economy grows normally, we will have surplus of significant size. This is what you might call surpluses by stealth. The political climate probably does not allow explicit targeting of surpluses but the government will end up with surpluses unless we have an economic down-turn. You might call also this policy sensible Keynesianism because it means you run surpluses in normal or good times and you have deficits—small deficits—if we have a down-turn. This is opposed to actual Keynesianism of the past where governments tended to forget about the surplus part.

At the Royal Bank, we have estimated the likely size of the fiscal dividend using the assumption that the federal Government will aim for this string of balanced budgets. We have assumed four percent annual growth of nominal GDP, an interest rate of seven percent and a contingency reserve of $3 billion. In addition, we assume that revenue grows at the same rate as GDP and program spending goes up with inflation and population. Under these assumptions, the fiscal dividend stars out small but then gets big. It will reach about $8 billion by the end of this government's mandate in 2001.

In considering spending and tax cuts, we have assumed that the government adheres to the Red Book formula and applies one-half of

141

the fiscal dividend to spending increases. Under this assumption, the ratio of program spending relative to GDP remains more or less flat. The other point I would make is that the program spending projected for next year relative to GDP will be lower than it has been since 1948, about 50 years ago.

If we add interest payments to the federal government's program spending, spending becomes much larger. But, because of the projected growth in GDP and reduced interest payments on the falling debt, in 2006 the ratio of total spending to GDP will be the lowest since the mid-1960s. Program spending by all levels of government, federal, provincial and local—in spite of off-loading—is presently at about one-third of GDP, the lowest level since the late 1970s. Total spending by all levels of government is about 43 percent now, down from its peak of 50 percent just a couple of years ago.

Focusing on the federal Government alone, is this level of spending too high or too low? I would suggest that there is no answer to this question. There are arguments that, if government gets too large, there are large disincentive effects of higher taxes and so on upon the economy. But, for the federal Government today the principal answer to the question in a society such as ours comes at the ballot box. It is principally a political rather than an economic question. During the last election, one party, the NDP, wanted bigger government and higher taxes. If I interpret them correctly, the Conservatives and the Reform wanted lower taxes and smaller government. The Liberals were somewhere in between and they won. So, it seems to me as an economist that at least within reasonable bounds the question of bigger or smaller government is principally determined by voters on the basis of their political attitudes and ideology.

But, let us suppose that it has been determined politically that taxes should be cut. What taxes should be cut? Let me consider just two contenders: the first is the EI premium and the second is income tax. If we decide to cut income taxes, there is a question about the precise nature of these cuts.

The case for cuts in employment insurance premiums is quite powerful, given the large accumulated surplus in the account. Some regard it as immoral, others as illegal. It is also said to be a tax on jobs. That claim is possibly true but it is not a watertight argument. Its truth depends on the incidence of EI premiums. If it is primarily on the worker, it will not much affect the cost of labour to employers. My reading of the evidence suggests that the incidence is mainly, at least in the longer term, on workers. So it is not clear quite how much of this is a tax on jobs. However, a good argument can be made in that high EI premiums raise unemployment in the short run.

If we compare cuts in income taxes with reductions in EI premiums and social insurance contributions, it is possible to approach the subject in another way. Total social security taxes as a percent of GDP in Canada are the lowest among the G7 countries. On the other hand, personal income taxes as a percent of GDP in Canada are the highest of the G7 countries. These figures suggest that a cut in personal income taxes may be more appropriate than cuts in the EI and other payroll taxes.

Canada has lower payroll taxes but much higher personal income taxes than the United States. This difference may be a source of problems for the Canadian economy and adds a further argument in favour of cuts in income taxes over cuts to payroll taxes. I cannot offer here a resolution of the conflicting arguments about the merit of cuts in different types of taxes. My main purpose it to suggest that the issues are not as simple as they might appear at first glance.

How might a cut in income taxes be carried out? Marginal tax rates in Canada do not form a smoothly increasing function of income. Instead, the relationship has some peaks and valleys. Those who pay the highest marginal income tax rates in Canada (60 percent or more) are not the rich but the people whose incomes are between $25,000 and $35,000. Why is this so? As you know, we provide financial support to very low income earners through such methods as GST rebates and child subsidies. As incomes rise, these benefits are clawed back quite quickly, making for very high implicit marginal rates of taxation.

I would like to make a case, then, for cuts in marginal income tax rates, starting at the bottom and then going to higher rates. Such a policy can be defended on grounds of both efficiency and fairness. A lot of people would agree that high marginal tax rates, over 50 percent, have disincentive effects on the rich and the poor. People on welfare often have marginal tax rates above 80 percent or even 90 percent. These rates are a real disincentive to getting off welfare. Working, low-income people similarly face these high marginal tax rates.

The equity case for such cuts in marginal rates stems from the fact that in the last decade or so the rich have got richer and the poor have got poorer—inequality has increased. This divergence in income is due mostly to technological factors that resulted in a reduction in the demand for unskilled people across all industrial countries, including Canada. Some federal programs (like the child tax credit) directed to lower income people try to adjust for these developments. Other efforts should be made to lower the high marginal tax rates on the moderately low income groups.

On the other hand, a good case could also be made for attacking the high marginal tax rates for people with high incomes. This case would rest on concerns about the brain drain to the United States, a phenomenon that affects more high income than low income earners.

In conclusion, let me restate that it is absolutely critical that the balanced budget targets be met—come hell or high water. Given that we have reached this goal, there will be a rising fiscal dividend. I would argue that the proportions of this dividend that should go to social programs, tax cuts, or debt reductions definitely should be decided on the basis of some economic criteria. However, ultimately the choice of these proportions is at least as much a question for the electorate as for economists. I think that cuts to EI premiums and income tax rates are good targets and that a public debate should take place about the nature of the income tax cut, especially the relative merit of cutting marginal tax rates for those with low and high incomes.

View of the Canadian Chamber of Commerce

TIM REID

The views in this chapter are the 1997 policy positions of the Canadian Chamber of Commerce. On December 2, 1997, we held a meeting of the entire Board of Directors, where we discussed the resolutions we passed at annual meetings in Saskatoon the previous September. These resolutions related to the fiscal policy issues discussed at the Fraser Institute Conference, *How to Spend the Fiscal Dividend: What is the Optimal Size of Government?* and this chapter will give you an idea of the kind of advice that the Chamber would like to give the government.

The Canadian Chamber of Commerce believes that before any decisions are made on the allocation of anticipated surpluses, we must pause and reflect. The battle to balance the budget was not fought so that Canada could enjoy a fiscal surplus for a year or two, but rather to set Canada on a long-term course of increased growth and prosperity with enhanced opportunity and security for all. It is in this context that we must assess our options.

We need to develop a framework within which we can determine what combination of policy actions, spending increases, tax reductions, and debt reductions are most likely to enhance Canada's competitive position and future economic growth. Without such a framework, there is a danger that less desirable proposals will be implemented and it is in this context that we should have strong concerns with the government's announced target of 50 percent of any surplus being applied to spending. This runs the risk that spending will take place in areas that contribute little to our future prosperity at the expense of other more beneficial efforts. I suggest there are five elements to this framework: (1) anchoring the gains, (2) accountability targets, (3) prudent assumptions, (4) tax reduction, and (5) criteria for program spending.

Anchoring the gains

Before the government undertakes any significant spending measures, it should securely anchor our fiscal gains. This means, first and foremost, reducing that debt load, which will not only reinforce confidence in Canada but will serve to reduce our current massive debt servicing costs of $43 billion over the long run and increase fiscal flexibility. Even with low interest rates, in 1997 the Federal Government spending on interest payments alone was 32 cents of every revenue dollar that could be used for other purposes. Reducing that debt load has to be the long term issue.

Accountability targets

The Federal Government's first mandate accomplishment has been aided in a substantial measure by the publication of targets for a fixed annual-deficit-to-GDP rate. In adopting this approach, the government drew a line in the sand on which rested the credibility of our fiscal policy. Outcomes consistently exceeded expectations, the government's credibility soared, Canada's credibility soared, interest rates fell, and a virtuous circle took root, speeding the elimination of the deficit. It is precisely because that approach was so effective that one must voice concern over the apparent lack of definition in the government's present fiscal strategy.

The notional fiscal dividend is ill defined, and its prospective division among competing objectives has been arbitrarily decided. Canadians in the international marketplace are left without any clear milestones whereby to assess progress along our new fiscal path. Indeed, we have as yet no developed concept of what our desired destination should be.

The Canadian Chamber of Commerce believes that some form of accountability targets should be a part of the government's new fiscal framework designed for the era of budget surpluses. These new targets would replace the rolling two-year deficit targets that now work so well. The targets could take the form of debt-to-GDP ratios or—what I think personally is more interesting—targets set according to the ratio to GDP of interest payments on the federal debt.

Prudent assumptions

Projected surpluses are highly sensitive, as we all know, to many factors. We therefore urge the government to continue the practice of applying prudent assumptions in its budget projections. At the 1997 APEC meetings in Vancouver, I attended the CEO summit and listened to views of CEOs about the dramatic economic events in Asia. As a result, I suggest that it is important to adhere to very prudent assumptions about economic growth in the next budget.

Tax reduction

The new fiscal framework should be aimed at reducing the job-killing and incentive-crushing tax burden. Canadians now prefer the speedy reduction of the debt-to-GDP ratio, which is consistent with tax cuts in the longer run. For the longer term, the Chamber calls for a new vision of government's appropriate role with respect to all its activities, but with particular focus on tax and transfer policy issues.

The criteria for judging program spending

The last report but one of the Auditor General stated that many government programs have no clear objective and no means to measure success against any criteria. In this light, does it make any sense that the government would pre-commit to spend one-half of the expected surplus? If any of the spending is on new programs, will these programs also not have clear and measurable objectives? If they are existing programs without clear rationales, is it not possible to prioritize the list of new activities and perhaps fund the worthy ones through the elimination of those programs that cannot demonstrate greater relative utility. The Canadian Chamber believes that all government programs, new and existing, should be tested against clear criteria.

In the 1970s, I was the Assistant Secretary, Effectiveness Evaluation Division, Treasury Board of Canada and then I was promoted to be Deputy Secretary of the Treasury Board Responsible for Efficiency Evaluation. I am still waiting to see the results of the work I did in these positions.

The current transition to a surplus era provides Canadians with an historic opportunity to reconsider whether the past 20 to 30 years of growth in government spending and taxation has provided a sound payoff. In terms of Finance Minister Paul Martin's stated criteria, the question is whether it has created a strong society and an economy characterized by opportunity and security.

The simple emergence of a fiscal surplus does not imply that additional spending is desirable and that such spending would improve general economic and social welfare. In light of this fact, a 50/50 allocation is strictly arbitrary. The plan to spend one-half the projected surplus assumes that the federal Government is not currently spending enough. Enough to support employment growth? Enough to provide essential services that can be best provided by the Federal Government? Enough to foster long-term economic growth? There are many who would argue that, notwithstanding the recent cuts, government spending still accounts for far too high a proportion of Canadian gross domestic product. At the very least, the government should facilitate the public determination of what the appropriate level should be, rather than arbitrarily presuming the increase to be good.

The role of government

Any emerging budgetary surplus should primarily be allocated to the reduction of the national debt and to tax reductions in order to establish Canada as one of the most dynamic global economies. IMF statistics paint a stark picture of Canada's global position with respect to government spending and taxation. Government spending in Canada as a percentage of GDP was almost 45 percent in 1996, which is about the average of the 17 major industrialized countries. However, our spending is far in excess of that of our neighbour, the United States. There is no question that Canada has a very large government sector but there are real doubts whether the accomplishment of the government's missions requires it to be so large. For example, low government spending and low unemployment rates are perfectly compatible. It can be argued that low spending may actually be a cause of low unemployment.

Tax policies

The positions of the Canadian Chamber of Commerce on taxation are determined at annual meetings of representatives from 500 Chambers of Commerce across the country through debates and votes on policy resolutions. So the Chamber positions are not thought up by myself nor a select committee of experts; they genuinely represent the views of businesses across Canada and are derived through intensive grassroots contacts as well as the input of an economic policy committee and a taxation committee made up of some of the best business economists in this country.

Positions we have taken have implications for the federal debt and they must be seen as a hierarchy of priorities. This hierarchy begins with the need to reduce our debt-to-GDP ratio substantially and quickly and, therefore, the expenditures of interest on that debt (which is the proper definition of a "fiscal dividend"). Then, there is the need for reductions on the job-killing EI premiums over the next two years. Chamber members, small businesses, and large businesses in all parts of the country believe that, if there was a significant reduction in EI over the next two years, more people would be hired because the cost of labour relative to the cost of other inputs would have been lowered. Moreover, reductions in employment insurance rates has the added advantage that it appeals to Canadians' sense of fairness. The EI premium is a fixed rate that applies only to the first $39,000 income. Therefore, by definition, it is a regressive tax whose burden falls disproportionately on those Canadians with low incomes and who are most vulnerable.

Beyond reductions in debt and EI premium rates, the Canadian Chamber proposes the lowering of the tax load on its citizens. Canadians have seen their tax load rise significantly over the years as a result of high EI premiums, hikes in CPP payments, higher effective tax rates through bracket creep and outright tax increases. As the federal Government gradually regains fiscal flexibility, it should consider the following specific changes in taxation: increases in the basic personal and spousal tax credits, restoration of full indexing of personal exemptions and brackets to inflation, restoration of the RRSP contribution limits to the level proposed many years ago, the elimination of the 3 percent surtax on high income earners. The latter tax was, in any event, intended as only as a temporary measure.

View of CIBC Wood Gundy

Jeffrey Rubin

I do not believe that massive surpluses will arise in the very distant future. I believe that we will see potentially massive surpluses in the very near term. While the Finance Minister has officially targeted a balanced budget for next year, it is pretty clear from the fiscal numbers to date that it will be achieved in the current 1997/1998 fiscal year. There may actually be a small surplus.

Revenues are about $10 billion ahead of plan, program spending is once again running below plan, and public-debt charges are right now tracking about $2 billion lower than the budget estimates. So, in fact, the most conservative assumptions would be that we would have a balanced budget this year and we may have a surplus of as much as $10 billion in the upcoming fiscal year, 1998/99.

I believe that under the guise of eliminating a phantom budget deficit, the Finance Minister will ward off calls for both tax cuts and government spending increases. He will effectively let the system crank out surpluses for this year and possibly 2 or 3 more years in the future. What the Finance Minister cannot achieve through political consensus at the Cabinet table, he will achieve through prudent budgetary assumptions.

As a result of such prudent assumptions, the deficit fell five times as much as was planned last year and produced a $15 billion overshoot of the deficit reduction target. In fact, a $10 billion surplus next year would not be even as large an overshoot as what he has achieved last year. Furthermore, the Finance Minister has already served notice in his Fall 1997 update that any future overshoots in deficit reduction would go directly to paying down the debt. So, in effect, the debate on how to utilize the surplus will begin only after the first $9 billion to $10 billion of that surplus is already used for debt reduction. This represents a *de facto* victory for debt reduction against competing uses of the fiscal dividend, be they government spending increases or tax cuts.

However, I do not believe that, beyond 1998/99, the government will make further debt reduction payments of that size without addressing those competing uses of the surplus. By that time, surpluses will already become apparent and it will be clear that they will grow exponentially. Even if growth of nominal GDP averaged 4 percent over the next four years, which is no greater than the lackluster performance of the last four years, the present fiscal system is primed to pump out very large surpluses. They would grow from roughly $9 billion or $10 billion next year to as much as $21 billion over the next four years, resulting in a cumulative surplus of $60 billion during the Liberal's second mandate.

I can guarantee one thing: someone will spend that money because there is no political support on either side of the political spectrum for governments running surpluses of such magnitude. The major cause of the projected surpluses is the growth in federal tax revenues in excess of economic growth.

Underlying this trend are built-in tax increases due to the absence of indexation of tax brackets and tax rates. Canadian taxpayers have been facing tax hikes since the mid-1980s when the indexation of personal exemptions and tax brackets was eliminated. They will do so in the future. Perversely, the reward for Canadian taxpayers for low inflation is a billion-dollar tax increase every year without any change in the schedule of rates. If average consumer-price inflation is 2 percent over the next four years, that means that there will be an effective tax hike of $4 billion at the federal level and, of course, a corresponding $2-billion tax hike for the provinces. If inflation were to rise to 3 percent, the automatic tax hike could be as large as $6 billion federally and $3.6 billion provincially.

It is important to note that the projected huge government surpluses require no further cuts in government spending. In our modeling exercise from which these projections are derived, we have allowed program spending beyond 1998/99 to grow by about 3.2 percent per year, reflecting inflation and population growth. In other words, we are allowing real per capita program spending to be preserved at the 1998/99 levels. This is a fairly generous assumption, given that over the last four years real per capita spending has fallen by about 20 percent. In addition, there is probably more flexibility for government spending than is implied by our assumptions. Payments of employment insurance claims are running between $2 billion and $3 billion less than budgeted in the fiscal plan. These funds will be available for reallocation to new spending initiatives without affecting the total level of program expenditures.

Lastly, the scale of debt reduction and the reduced borrowing needs insulate the federal government from the very large increases in debt servicing costs that plagued the federal Government in the late l980s and early 1990s. So, even with as much as a 200-basis-point rise in interest rates throughout the yield curve over the next four years, we will not see very much movement in debt servicing costs.

The federal Government has said that it will use 50 percent of the fiscal dividend to increase government spending. We have estimated that this policy would result in an unprecedented increase in government spending. It would result in a $9 billion increase in spending in 1998/99. Such an increase would wipe out all of the spending restraint of the last three budgets. Over the three-year period from 1999/2000 to 2001/02, spending would increase over $20 billion annually. Spending in the future would grow at 6 percent per year. It should be remembered that such spending increases could take place while budgets remain balanced and there are no explicit tax increases.

Alternatively, if 50 percent of the projected surpluses were allocated to tax cuts, these could equal a $3 billion a year in each of the next four years, commencing in the next budget. That would accumulate to a little over $13 billion annually at the end of the period. Even with these tax cuts, the government would still post modest surpluses of about $5 billion to $6 billion a year, which, in turn, would accumulate to a debt reduction of about $24 billion. The debt-to-GDP ratio would decline from near 73 percent in 1997 to about 53 percent, reversing all of the fiscal deterioration since the 1990s.

What about the notion that the projected surplus be allocated totally to debt reduction? The American experience suggests that this is not likely to take place for political reasons. Even during very prosperous times in 1997, with unemployment at a 25-year low, all prospective surpluses were quickly spent by Congress and the Administration. There was no political will to run a budgetary surplus.

In both the Republican and Democratic camp, budget surpluses ran a very distant second to alternative fiscal uses. In the Republican camp, tax cuts came first, with capital gain tax cuts on the top of the list. For the Democrats, government spending increases came first, with priority going to spending on education. I find it hard to believe that in Canada with 9.1 percent unemployment, the public will endorse debt reduction of a very aggressive scale.

I believe it is important to compare Canadian with foreign rates of taxation. Although we hear a lot about substantial increases in CPP premiums over the next four to five years, in fact Canada has the lowest indirect taxes as a percentage of GDP in the entire G7, including the United States. Alternatively, personal income taxes as a share of GDP in Canada are by far the highest.

Personal income taxes in Canada are also at an all-time high historically. Even a tax cut of $3 billion a year, or $13 billion over four years would just restore the ratio of personal income tax to GDP to its level in 1988. This level, in turn, is still much higher than it was at the beginning of the 1980s.

Why has the issue of tax cuts attracted so little public attention in recent times? There are two fundamental reasons. First, until recently people very much believed Paul Martin's deficit numbers; I think many among my colleagues on Bay Street still do. This pessimistic view on deficits ruled out tax cuts. I think that this was a proper attitude then, but now that it is increasingly realized that the deficits are actually turning into surpluses, tax cuts are getting discussed more and more. I am convinced that the case for cuts will win.

Second, there has been a failure in the political arena to bring up the subject of tax cuts in the proper context. The very people who advocated tax cuts in the last election, specifically the Reform Party and the Progressive Conservatives, played Paul Martin's game by accepting his forecasts for continued deficits. As a result, they were forced to endorse large cuts in government spending in order to pay for tax cuts. Canadians quite rightly thought that they did not want to endure any further cuts in government spending and accompanying closures of hospitals and schools. These closures were not worth to them a small reduction in their personal income taxes.

The reality is that the public was offered a false choice. There was no need for spending reductions to finance tax cuts. The real issue was whether the pace of deficit reduction would be tripled or quadrupled or whether Canadian taxpayers would share in some of these fiscal benefits.

Looking forward, I believe that Canadians do not want ideological arguments about the optimum size of government. They fear that they might lead to more years of painful program spending cuts. I believe that Canadians now realize that the choice is between surpluses and tax cuts. Once faced with this choice, I have confidence that Canadians will choose to reform a tax system that penalizes efficiency, confiscates purchasing power, and undermines competitiveness.

Discussion of Views of Business Economists

Editor's Note: The following draws on a transcript of a round-table discussion that took place after the presentations by John McCallum, Tim Reid, and Jeffrey Rubin. I have edited all questions and answers heavily to make them brief and concise, and I apologize for the omission of much wit, repartee, and rhetoric that brightened the live proceedings. The participants have given their approval of the edited version of their remarks.

Question 1

Michael Walker   I have some questions that link the presentations by the business economists with the papers by the economists in the first session. According to Ludger Schuknecht, the empirical evidence strongly suggests that there are no benefits from government expenditures beyond 30 percent of GDP. Spending above this level does not increase school enrolment, life expectancy, or even income distribution. Gerald Scully pointed out that economic growth is reduced by tax rates above what he refers to as the optimal level. David Giles noted that the underground economy begins to swell as tax rates rise above a certain level.

Therefore I wonder what makes John McCallum say that economists have nothing to say about what the size of government should be. Surely the choice of an optimal size of government is not just ideological; it is not one just to be decided at the ballot box. It is important that the people know about the consequences of increased spending, that beyond a certain level of spending there will be few improvements in health, education, and life expectancy, and that it is likely to reduce economic growth.

Response

John McCallum   I do not think I said economists had nothing to say. I said I think that, within limits, it is principally a political issue when it comes to income distribution. Ludger Schuknecht notes that income distribution is more equal when transfers and subsidies are higher. Economists from Queen's University in Kingston compared the increase in inequality over the last several years in the United States and Canada. They found that the increase in inequality in terms of wage incomes was about the same, maybe slightly more in the United States than in Canada. However, once the Canadians tax and transfer system is taken into account, inequality in Canada had not increased significantly.

I accept that the tax and transfer system has had negative effects on incentives and economic growth in Canada. Therefore, Canada relative to the United States had a lower rate of economic growth but gained a greater equality of income. The trade-off between growth and equality is the kind of issue which I would suggest can only be settled through the political process.

Comment

Michael Walker   I agree with your basic proposition that such a trade-off between growth and income equality involves ethical judgements. But, I would insist that they also have an empirical dimension. Consider that in 1965, 4.7 percent of income before tax went to the lowest quintile of income earners in Canada. In 1995, that quintile's share had risen to 5.4 percent. This improvement of one percentage point in the income going to the bottom quintile was achieved through an increase of spending from 30 percent to 45 percent of GDP. This is the kind of information economists can bring to the public decision making process, even if, at bottom, it involves ethical judgements that are resolved through the political process.

John McCallum   My personal view is that we made a mistake raising the size of government as much as you indicated. We agree on that point. My main contention is that the present size of the federal Government is the lowest in 50 years and that we do not want it necessarily to be smaller than that.

Question 2

Audience   I have seen the economic forecasts today and am reminded of my work at the Economic Council of Canada before it was dissolved. We made the same sort of simulations around 1990 and produced the same results. Very large surpluses would appear in just 3 or 4 years. We all know that these surpluses did not develop. There was this little matter of the 1991 recession that we had not put into our simulations. This experience leads me to suggest that it is risky to count the chickens before they are hatched—to plan tax reductions or spending or spending increases before the surplus is realized. The business cycle has not been repealed and we could have a recession before too long.

Answer

Jeffrey Rubin   I think that it would be spurious to model a recession for a specific year in the future. All one can do in such modeling is to assume that the future four years will be much like the last four years in terms of economic growth and its effect on tax revenue and spending. Canada's nominal 4 percent average annual growth rate from 1990 to 1996 has not exactly been spectacular. So, forecasting an average 4 percent nominal GDP growth in the next four years could easily accommodate a recession as long there would be a recovery afterwards, which would be the normal case in any business cycle.

Let me note that the improvement in the fiscal balances, which in recent years has been two to three times faster than forecast by anyone—including the Department of Finance—was not driven by economic growth. It has mainly been driven by a combination of spending cutbacks and tax increases. Such tax increases will allow federal revenues to continue to grow faster than the 4 percent at which we expect nominal GDP to grow. This is due to the absence of indexation of the taxation system, which will generate an extra $6 billion in federal revenue over the next four years. More favourable fiscal outlooks could be obtained if, for example, we used the Bank of Canada's assumption that the economy would grow at 4 percent in real terms, a nominal growth closer to 6 percent.

Tim Reid   I agree basically with Jeffrey Rubin's reply but I am concerned about the impact of the Asian flu, especially after I listened to government leaders at the recent APEC conference in Vancouver. In comparison, here in Canada we have some of our fundamentals right, but it is important to stay with conservative assumptions in making forecasts.

John McCallum   My estimates are similar to Jefftey Rubin's, but there are some differences in the interpretation. I agree that the federal Government probably is in balance this year. My estimate of the fiscal dividends could afford a tax cut of $3 billion in each of the next four years, but I do not think we should embark on that road too soon. I was in Vancouver too, and it is scary. It is really scary. We do not know what will happen in Asia. Anything could happen. I personally think the impact on us will be limited but there is a risk that it could get out of hand. There is also the risk that the Quebec issue could get out of hand, especially with the election there coming up in 1998. Political events are much harder to predict than economic developments.

I do not want the Federal Government to commit itself in the next budget to a long string of substantial tax cuts when there will have been only one year at best of a balanced budget or a small surplus. If everything goes well and there are surpluses of $7 billion or $8 billion in 1998/99, it is not a catastrophe if these funds are used to reduce the debt.

Question 3

Audience   I am concerned about the government's unfunded liabilities through the Canada Pension Plan and about the prospect of much higher medical expenses as the population ages. Is the government not in fact in a much worse situation than it looks on book? And, if that is the case, should paying down the debt not be given a very high priority?

Answer

John McCallum   The biggest single reason for attaching a very high priority to getting the debt-to-GDP ratio down over the next 10 to 15 years is the large number of baby boomers reaching retirement age. Therefore the present grace period of 10, 12, or 15 years should be used to pay down the debt. On the CPP, I would say that it is in good shape now. Whether you like the way the government has dealt with it or not, it has been put on a solvent footing by those premium increases.

Jeffrey Rubin   There is no doubt that we have to reduce the debt relative to the economy. But this will occur automatically when the budget is balanced and the economy grows. I have been advocating that we should get the debt-to-GDP ratio lowered to around 53 percent. Economists do not know what the optimal debt-to-GDP ratio is. Most would agree that it should not be 73 percent. I think it is better to use growth in GDP rather than absolute debt reductions to get to a lower debt-to-GDP ratio. The surpluses needed to pay down the debt are not going to be politically acceptable.

It is important to note that the debt-to-GDP ratio will be the same in the future whether 50 percent of the projected surplus is used for increased government spending at 6 percent to 7 percent a year, or for equivalent tax cuts. In this sense, the debt-to-GDP ratio is a red herring. The real issue is tax cuts or spending increases. I suggest we choose tax cuts.

Tim Reid   I think that for Canada's international competitiveness it is important to consider the way the country is perceived abroad. Foreign investors act on their perception of Canada's fiscal toughness. They are difficult to persuade by complex arguments of the sort Jeffrey Rubin just made. I think that we need to send a clear and unambiguous message that Canada is serious about its fiscal order by a simple commitment to debt reduction—that we will reach a debt-to-GDP ratio of, say, 60 percent by the year 2,000 at the very, very latest and appropriate downward targets thereafter. I think that such a policy would help bring into Canada more of the foreign investment that now is going to the United States, in spite of the fact that we have many of our fundamentals right.

Comment

Michael Walker   Regarding Tim Reid's comment, let me just remind you that in this morning's session it was noted that the rate of taxation for capital gains is 20 percent in the United States and 40 percent in Canada in some provinces. Investors in high-tech industries get most of their returns through capital gains. Therefore it should really not come as a surprise that Canada fails to attract the level of high-tech investment that all of us think we should have. While there is also a large gap in the personal income tax favouring the United States, I think that in the field of high-tech investment the government could achieve most by a lowering of the capital gains tax rate.

John McCallum   I certainly think that it would help Canada if we had lower capital gains tax and lower income tax. But, I also think marketing is a crucial policy. Canada ranks very high in objective rankings of countries like those prepared by organizations like the World Economic Forum and the Economist's Intelligence Unit. Yet, on more subjective evaluations like those of the Chief Executive Officer in The World Economic Forum Canada ranks much lower. This problem should be addressed by appropriate marketing of Canada, conveying the message that we are open for business and that we have a lot of good things going for us.

On the point of capital gains, I agree that we need to narrow the gap between the Canadian and American rates. If we want to get lower unemployment and more jobs, we need to attract capital and small companies. They are the engines of job creation and they are discouraged from coming to Canada because of the high tax rates.

Question 4

Audience   I wonder what the economic analysts foresee for monetary policy in Canada as the fiscal situation moves from deficits to potentially large surpluses and cuts in income taxes and as the economy closes the existing output gap.

Answer

Jeffrey Rubin   I think we are a long way from closing the output gap in Canada by the fourth quarter of 1998. At a 9.1 percent unemployment rate, we are far from full employment. Inflationary pressures are much beyond short-term forecasting horizons. Wage inflation is unlikely to develop before the unemployment rate reaches 7 percent, which will not occur until we have created another 800,000 to 900,000 new jobs.

The Bank of Canada has now lost control of monetary policy because of concerns with the foreign exchange market. I think its forecast for 4 percent real economic growth is threatened by the developments in the money and foreign exchange markets. However, it is clear that if, against my expectation, Canada would have substantial fiscal surpluses, monetary policy would have to become easier.

John McCallum   I agree with Jeffrey Rubin that Canada is a long way from an output gap of zero. The Asian crisis and the weaker world commodity prices make for lower future growth and even smaller prospects that the output gap will be closed soon.

On monetary policy, I would note that the monetary rule now followed by the Bank of Canada implies smaller fiscal multipliers in either direction than has been the case in the past. As the Bank of Canada targets a certain growth rate of the overall economy and has a certain view of how fast it wants the economy to grow, the impact of a tax cut or a tax increase on spending will be less than it was before.

Comment

Filip Palda   John McCallum said that the optimal size of a government is probably a political question, and I think he was right. It should be the consumers of government services who decide in the end. The problem in Canada is that these consumers cannot express their views except in an elections once every four years. Maybe one way to get at the optimal size of government would be to give these consumers more ways of choosing their product: decentralization of government responsibilities, more use of referendums and greater use of user fees.

Views of the Federal
Political Parties

View of the Reform Party

PRESTON MANNING

We are now well into this discussion of where to go once the budget is balanced and this question has preoccupied our thinking for the last number of months. In particular, we have been concerned with whether there are optimal levels of government, taxation, and debt, which ought to guide us once we get beyond the balanced budget. Reform's thinking on this subject is contained in a discussion paper called *Beyond A Balanced Budget*. Monte Solberg, our finance critic and Jason Kenney, our revenue critic, are in the process of consolidating what they learned from our consultations on that subject.

Here is a short outline of our thinking at this time. On the size of government, we are convinced that there is such a thing as an optimal size of government—that, if government spending, activities, and taxation exceed some percentage of GDP, they become counterproductive. We believe that this optimum level of government is somewhere in the vicinity of 30 percent of GDP for Canada, which is a long way below where we are now.

With respect to debt reduction and tax relief, we fundamentally disagree with the government that the first priority for the use of the fiscal dividend should be increased spending. We are conscious every day in the House that the Liberals have an instinctive desire to spend and tax. Maybe this desire is in their genes or chromosomes or something because it is genetic and certainly not rational.

In the throne speech, the Liberals made a commitment to spend 50 percent of any surplus and put 50 percent toward debt reduction and tax relief. But immediately thereafter, they made 29 proposals for additional spending. There were no concrete ideas about debt reduction or tax cuts. We are conscious of the fact that when the Liberals are confronted with any kind of problem, whether it is the deficit, global warming, or problems with the CPP, their instinctive reaction is to tax to solve the problem.

Reform's instincts are fundamentally different. Our instinct is first of all to limit the growth in government spending to 6 percent to keep up with the growth in GDP and population. Half of the surplus beyond that will be used for debt reduction and half for tax relief. We acknowledge that a case can be made for increased investment in certain areas, perhaps in health care, research, and development or post-secondary education. However, we believe that these needs should be met through the re-allocation of budgets within the existing envelopes rather than through additional spending.

With respect to a debt reduction target, we are pleased to see groups like the C.D. Howe Institute and the Fraser Institute calling on governments to promote responsible approaches to debt reduction and to set targets. The Prime Minister has set a target for reduction of CO_2 emissions. We would encourage him to carry on into the area of debt reduction. We support these proposals that have come from the think tanks. I would be interested to know whether there was anything presented this morning that should lead us to re-examine Reform's aim at long range of getting the debt to GDP ratio to the 20 percent to 25 percent range within 20 years.

With respect to tax relief, in the 1997 election we campaigned on the vision of a leaner, smaller, efficient government, a focused federal Government, and a significant reduction in taxes. Our "fresh start" tax-relief package included a reduction of about $3 billion in the EI premiums paid by Canada's employers and a reduction of $12 billion in personal income taxes through a variety of measures—increasing the personal exemption, the spousal exemption, some changes in the child care tax deduction, and a 50 percent reduction in capital gains tax. We are pleased that a Liberal-dominated Finance Committee has stolen a number of our ideas on tax relief, and we hope that the government does take our advice on some of these recommendations. It is funny that when we put these things out during the election campaign they were called tax cuts for the rich, even though we took about 1.3 million lower- and middle-income tax payers off the tax roll altogether; but now that they are reproduced in the Liberal document, they are called "Responsible Proposals for Tax Relief."

The challenge for the Fraser Institute now is to provide the intellectual foundation for moving beyond the balanced budget and communicating that foundation as effectively as possible to opinion leaders. In the political arena, I see the Reform Party facing a communications challenge and a credibility challenge. With respect to communications challenge, we have a huge job to acquaint the public—and I mean large numbers of people who ultimately vote—with the dangers and costs of high debt and high taxes. We intend to hammer away on the themes that the high debt is bad, fiscally and socially, the latter because the interest cost on a high debt erodes our capacity to finance social programs.

We will also hammer away on the simple fact that taxes kill jobs. People want to know why the unemployment rate is so high presently. One of the reasons is that we are just not leaving enough dollars in the pockets of consumers to spend and of business to invest. We will also stress one of the positive benefits to the public of debt and tax relief. It is the shortest way to higher disposable income, more jobs, and getting more stable financing for social programs.

With respect to the second challenge, I think it imperative that we be credible on this subject, which is why your research is so important. We will get the public's ear on this subject of debt reduction and debt targets, and we will get their ear on tax relief, but we better be right in what we say. We cannot afford a debate in Canada like that in the United States on the flat tax. In that debate, the disagreements among the advocates of different versions of the tax damaged the basic idea more than the comments of the critics.

At the provincial level, I suggest that Premiers like Ralph Klein and Mike Harris are credible on this subject, and will be credible because they practise what they preach with respect to balanced budgets. At the federal level, there is a credibility problem, because the Liberals did not use the opportunity to balance the budget and reduce the debt and taxes when they first came to office. In fact, they did exactly the opposite. They ran up an even higher debt by running deficits in excess of $40 billion and raised taxes 71 times. There is a sobering lesson for all of us in this. Professed ideological conservatives in the academic community and political arena, no matter what our political stripe, can lose credibility. It is especially possible to lose it, if we fail to deliver on the principles and our commitments.

Reform is now the official opposition to the government. This gives us the opportunity to become the most credible federal advocate for federal debt reduction and tax relief. We intend to take advantage of this opportunity. We have carried the ball on deficit reduction in Parliament since 1993, and we now intend to carry the ball on debt reduction and tax relief until the goal line is crossed.

View of the New Democratic Party

Nelson Riis

When I was first elected in 1980, Tommy Douglas sat me down with a number of others and gave us very practical advice. He told us "Debts and deficits are very bad things. When you are beholden to bankers, you cannot do the things that you want to do as Social Democrats." Today the high government debt prevents us from having the social programs the NDP wants.

When pre-budget hearings in Vancouver began in the Fall of 1997, Paul Martin, the Minister of Finance indicated that the government had cut up its credit card. They had wrestled the deficit to the ground. This remark made me think how easy it is to cut up your credit card when you ask other people to use theirs, because this is what the federal government has done by off-loading its financial problems on other levels of government, on students and their families who have to pay more for education, on sick Canadians waiting in long lineups, and on families who face the increased costs of caring for their elderly parents and children.

This off-loading of the deficit should stop us from feeling smug about the attainment of a balanced budget. The Minister of Finance keeps on saying that he had no other way of dealing with the deficit; I will simply say that he is categorically wrong. There were other alternatives. Janice MacKinnon has described the ways in which Saskatchewan dealt with a very serious deficit and debt issue. They made the needed hard choices but they did not reduce the funding to social programs and health care. As a matter of fact, they increased health-care spending by $100 million to make up for the cuts that the federal Government had imposed on them. At the same time they were fiscally prudent and were the first province to balance its budget.

Speaking for the NDP, I consider unacceptable the Liberal proposals that 50 percent of future budget surpluses should be used for increased program spending and 50 percent for debt reduction and tax relief. I think that Saskatchewan's decision to use one-third for spending increases, one-third for tax relief and one-third for debt reduction is appropriate for the federal government. Its much larger cuts in program spending and especially health care and education require devoting 50 percent of the surplus to spending increases to restore them to their needed levels.

However, I think it is important for the Fraser Institute and for ourselves as parliamentarians to work on credibility for our causes. It is not enough for us to talk about figures. We need also to talk about people. For example, I have two sons, aged 25 and 27. Recently we discussed the first food banks in Canada, established in Edmonton in 1989. Today there are over 900 food banks in Canada. Some food banks have large numbers of subsidiaries, like the main food bank in Toronto, which has 80 subsidiaries. There are more food banks than McDonald's and Wendy's put together. This story of the growth of food banks reveals a side of our society that should be included in the discussion of the topics that are discussed here today.

It is fair to say that while Canada has eliminated its fiscal deficit, it has created a massive social deficit. Unemployment has been running at over 9 percent now for 85 consecutive months. Nearly 400,000 young people are unemployed today. I do not think that we can stand by and accept those figures and not do anything significant about them immediately. There is a serious risk of major social economic upheavals in the future when 400,000 young men and women are unemployed at the time in their lives when they should be building their careers, homes, and families.

In 1989, Ed Broadbent moved a motion that by the year 2000 Canada eradicate child poverty. I seconded the motion, which passed unanimously in the House of Commons. Since 1989, we have 538,000 more children living in poverty in this country. There are now 1.5 million of them living in these conditions. I do not know your feelings on this issue but it concerns me very much, knowing about the importance of the first 3 years in the development of children. Psychologists and physicians tell us that the values, the ethics, the fundamentals of a person's character are created in these formative years. Living in poverty severely limits the future development of these children and prevents them from becoming productive citizens.

We do not have to accept Canadian children living in poverty. There are a number of countries in the world where child poverty does not exist simply because the parents of these children do not live in poverty. So, there are models that we can look to and adopt in Canada.

With respect to income, I learned the other day that over 89 percent of new jobs in Canada are created in the self-employment sector. In this sector, the average income is $20,000 per year. What does that mean for our capitalist economic system that depends on people having the ability to purchase goods and services when levels of income are so low and disposable income is so limited?

When we discuss the question of the optimal size of government, may I urge us first to spend some time discussing the purpose of government. What do we expect the governments of our country to do? What services do we expect them to provide?

I consider debt reduction to be a major issue facing Canada. Therefore, I was pleased to noted that the Finance Committee Report urged the continued application to debt reduction of all surpluses in the contingency reserve of annual budgets.

On a more general topic, I would like to say something which may surprise some people since it is coming from a social democrat. It is crucial that we find new ways and means of expanding wealth creation in Canada. We need to identify strategic investments that will make our economy grow. Finding expanding markets and selling in them is crucial.

I know it is very popular today to talk about the devolution of power. When Quebec asked for, and was given, the right to run its own manpower training programs, this right was granted to all provincial governments. I wonder whether it is necessarily in Canada's best interest to have 10 different systems of training. We now have an explosion in the number of training institutes. In the province of British Columbia there are now over a thousand training institutes, but only a hundred of them are certified. What kind of training are we doing? What are we doing in terms of ensuring some national standard across the country?

In summary, let me say that social democrats in the House of Commons and across the country will insist that we remain vigilant in terms of an efficient and effective government, that we no longer need to visit the old issue of deficits, that we continue to acknowledge the seriousness of debt. But we will also insist that we give some consideration, immediately and in the future, to rewarding those people that really fought and won the deficit war, the students of Canada with the high debt loads, people waiting in lineups in hospitals, the children living in poverty, and particularly those people who are unemployed.

View of the Progressive Conservative Party

THE HONOURABLE JEAN CHAREST

Politics is about teaching and each of us in our roles as politicians should take on that task and responsibility. We should not only put forward positions but also help to advance the public debate. This is true of the issue of the fiscal dividend. Today, most of us would recognize that we were ahead of our time in the 1997 election campaign. We talked about tax cuts, balancing the books, and the importance of reducing the debt. According to an Angus Reid poll (Globe and Mail / Angus Reid, November 1997), Canadians now agree with us on these problems. This confirms that if one is able to communicate and to be persuasive Canadians are ready to listen and change their views on these very important issues.

Let me start with a bit of a cold shower on the theme of this meeting. I disagree with the whole idea that there is a fiscal dividend. There is no fiscal dividend. If the truth be told, the government of Canada now is using the funds in the Employment Insurance Fund for the purpose of paying down the deficit and, by doing so, they are over-taxing Canadian workers and businesses for the purpose of meeting that objective. They are talking about a fiscal dividend of $12 billion to $13 billion when no fiscal dividend exists. Nevertheless, I do not

---

Please note that this speech was delivered by Jean Charest before he became leader of the Liberal Party of Quebec.

argue with the importance of us looking ahead. The fiscal dividend we hope for is on the horizon—is well within our reach—and it is extremely important for us to prepare for that moment so that we make the right choices.

It is interesting how this debate about the use of future surpluses has evolved since I was first elected in 1984. The entire issue of deficits and debts now transcends political ideologies. All levels of governments agree on it and there is a very broad and solid consensus in Canada. That was not always the case. Today we benefit from this consensus to the point where New Democrats in Saskatchewan and Liberals in New Brunswick and even the federal Liberals have all warmed up to the idea that we have to balance our books and start paying down debt.

The main question we now face is what we should do with surplus funds once the budget is balanced. Before we turn to the question of the optimal size of government, we should examine the role of government. Only after we have done the latter, can we link the two questions. I think that it is important that we examine these questions as Canadians, regardless of the choices made by the United States. I urge that we be on guard against importing wholesale political ideologies from other jurisdictions. We must remember that political ideology is not applied in a vacuum but rather in the context of our history and our culture and the choices that we make.

In this respect, if there is one conclusion that I have come to from my experience and travels of the last few years, it is that these deficits, debt, and high taxes run counter to our basic Canadian culture. If there is one conclusion that I have come to from the debates within our party and in spending time with Canadians, it is that we Canadians have always lived in a country where there was ample freedom to reap the rewards of work. Governments at all levels and formed by all political parties over the last few years got badly off track by allowing themselves to get into a spending spiral that created this debt and high taxes. We are now paying the price in terms of a lower standard of living and higher unemployment.

It is always risky to compare the Canadian economy with the American economy. Yet, I think we should ask ourselves why the United States has half the unemployment rate that we have and why its standard of living in the last four years has gone up while ours has gone down? In Canada, we have reduced disposable income and we have more poor children today than in 1993. If it had not been for the Canada-US Free Trade Agreement and the North American Free Trade Agreement, which were adopted during the last Progressive Conservative governments, our economy would have been in a recession.

I believe that these differences in the success of the Canadian and American economies are directly related to higher taxes and higher debt. For this reason, we continue to propose setting out some clear objectives for our fiscal framework. The Conservatives' position continues to be that taxes should be reduced now, immediately. We distinguish ourselves in this respect. We were the only party in the last campaign to take that position.

We have a logical reason for taking this position. As the Fraser Institute and others suggest, there is an optimal size of government that is reached when government spending equals 30 percent of GDP. Spending beyond that point results in negative returns. Since in Canada we have spending in excess of the critical 30 percent of GDP, spending reductions would increase productivity and government revenues. In the light of these facts, we were surprised that in the last election campaign that we were the only party proposing immediate tax reductions, before the books were balanced.

As a priority, cuts in payroll taxes rank very high for us. EI premiums are a tax on jobs—a circumstance which, quite frankly, is scandalous. Moreover, we find it morally objectionable to have a government lecture the people of eastern Canada about the abuse of the Employment Insurance system and then abuse it themselves. We believe that if there will be increases in CPP premiums, they should be matched by reductions in EI premiums so that Canadians do not face even higher taxes. We also believe in a reduction in personal income taxes. We think there should be a very clear target set for our debt-to-GDP ratio; we suggest a ratio of 50 percent by the year 2005.

We also believe that there is a need for a framework for reduced spending, lowering of the debt and deficit, and for tax reductions. We need to explain to Canadians that, if we make these reductions in spending and in the debt, there will be the reward of lower taxes. We called for tax cuts before the budget is balanced. Our position on the fiscal dividend is that one-third, at least, should be applied to debt reduction and the rest to meeting demographic spending needs and further tax cuts. However, the increased spending should be undertaken only within a system that guarantees benefits.

Let me conclude by giving you a reason why it is important that we move ahead with such fiscal plans. Young Canadians with skills for which there is a market anywhere in the world now have choices that Canadians a generation ago did not have. For example, when I graduated from Sherbrooke University in 1981 in law, it was not obvious that I would be able to work somewhere else in the world. But, today Canadian university graduates can take advantage of the new environment of globalization and can readily find jobs in other countries. This fact has important implications for the future of Canada. Consider that computer science graduates at the University of Waterloo in recent years have been courted successfully by many foreign employers. Microsoft Corporation alone hired one-third of all of these recent graduates.

What causes this brain drain? Graduates are attracted to higher pay and lower taxes. They do not have to stay behind to pay off the debt incurred by their parents. Some people say that such higher after-tax income does not compensate for the outstanding quality of life that we have here in Canada. Well, apparently these graduates do not see it that way: with enough extra income, that quality of life is accessible pretty much anywhere in the world. We must deal with this problem or suffer very serious long-term problems for our great country as young people choose to live and work elsewhere.